11/22

WHY HUMANS BUILD UP

The Rise of Towers, Temples and Skyscrapers

WHY HUMANS BUILD UP

The Rise of Towers, Temples and Skyscrapers

GREGOR CRAIGIE

Illustrated by
KATHLEEN FU

ORCA BOOK PUBLISHERS

Published in Canada and the United States in 2022 by Orca Book Publishers.
orcabook.com

Library and Archives Canada Cataloguing in Publication
Title: Why humans build up : the rise of towers, temples and skyscrapers / Gregor Craigie ; illustrated by Kathleen Fu.
Names: Craigie, Gregor, author. | Fu, Kathleen, illustrator.
Description: Series statement: Orca timeline ; 1 | Includes bibliographical references and index.
Identifiers: Canadiana (print) 20210352469 | Canadiana (ebook) 20210352485 |
ISBN 9781459821880 (hardcover) | ISBN 9781459827172 (PDF) | ISBN 9781459827189 (EPUB)
Subjects: LCSH: Tall buildings—Juvenile literature.
Classification: LCC NA6230 .C73 2022 | DDC j720/.483—dc23

Library of Congress Control Number: 2021948635

Summary: Part of the nonfiction Orca Timeline series, with photographs and illustrations throughout. This book explores
why and how people have constructed taller and taller buildings over the course of human history.

Orca Book Publishers is committed to reducing the consumption of nonrenewable resources in the production of our books.
We make every effort to use materials that support a sustainable future.

Orca Book Publishers gratefully acknowledges the support for its publishing programs provided
by the following agencies: the Government of Canada, the Canada Council for the Arts
and the Province of British Columbia through the BC Arts Council and the Book Publishing Tax Credit.

Author photo by Rebecca Craigie
Illustrator photo by Diego Zabala
Cover and interior artwork by Kathleen Fu
Design by Rachel Page
Edited by Kirstie Hudson

Printed and bound in Canada.

25 24 23 22 • 1 2 3 4

For Lochlan, Benji and Charlie,
who are always looking up and always asking, "Why?"

Contents

INTRODUCTION

I can still remember the first time I saw a *skyscraper*. I was five years old and sitting in the back seat of my dad's car. We drove over the top of a hill and I saw what looked like a giant white rocket, about half a mile (one kilometer) in front of us. It had a big red ring near the top and looked like a steel needle pointing straight up at the sky.

"What's that?" I asked.

"That's the Calgary Tower," my dad replied. "It's the tallest building in the city."

The tower was only five years older than me, and it looked modern, new and impossibly high. I pressed my cheek up against the glass as we drove past and tried to look straight up the long, smooth *concrete* cylinder. It was so high!

I peppered my dad with questions for the rest of the car ride and for weeks after. How tall is it? How did they make it? What's at the top? Will it fall over? The questions kept coming until he finally took me and my sister to visit the tower. The elevator took about a minute to lift us to the viewing deck, almost 620 feet (190 meters) above the ground. When we looked out the big windows I was amazed by the incredible views. I could see the tops of all the other big buildings surrounding the tower, thousands of houses beyond them and the spectacular Rocky Mountains off in the distance.

I have been interested in tall towers ever since that day. But it wasn't until I grew up and became a dad myself that I really started to wonder why we build them. I was showing my sons a photo of the Burj Khalifa—a skyscraper in Dubai that is four times taller than the Calgary Tower—when one of them asked me a simple question. "Why did they make it so high?"

That's a good question, and one that could be asked of every tall building that's ever been built.

One of the biggest reasons for going high today is because the world's population is growing. With more people, we will need more space for those people to live, learn and work in. At the same time, it's important to preserve what wilderness we have left, like the forests and jungles that provide habitat for endangered species and act as carbon sinks, removing the greenhouse gas carbon dioxide from the air.

But there are many more reasons why people have been building tall structures for centuries. Castle walls kept people on the inside safe. Utility towers transmitted television and mobile phone signals. And observatories gave people a bird's-eye view of what surrounded them. There are some good reasons for building up, and a few bad ones as well. But it's worth thinking more about why we're doing it, because it's safe to assume we will have to keep building higher in the future.

The Calgary Tower was built in the 1960s to celebrate Canada's centennial and bring tourists into Calgary's downtown core.

When it was first built, the 626-foot (191-meter) reinforced-concrete observation tower was the tallest building in Calgary. It's no longer the tallest, but it is still prominent on the city's skyline.
YÙ DÒU JIN YE / EYEEM/GETTY IMAGES

Tower of Jericho
8300 BCE

Lighthouse of Alexandria
280 BCE

One
SECURITY

BUILDING TALL TO STAY SAFE

Skyscrapers look like modern inventions, with striking vertical lines of glass and steel stretching high into the sky. Most **architects** and historians agree that the first skyscrapers were built in Chicago and New York in the late 1800s and most of the really high towers were built in the last few decades. But people have been building tall structures for thousands of years. And one of the very first reasons was for security—people built tall structures to keep themselves safe.

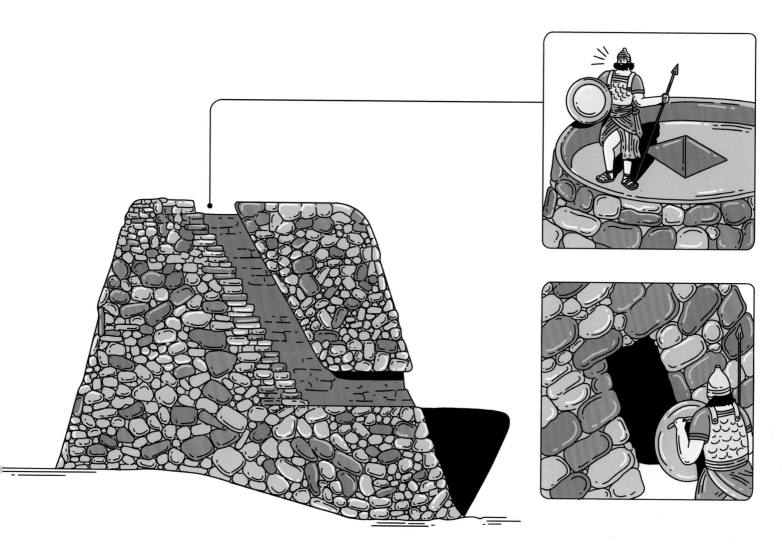

THE TOWER OF JERICHO

- *HEIGHT: 28 feet (8.5 meters)* • *YEAR FINISHED: About 8300 BCE*
- *LOCATION: Jordan River Valley*
- *MATERIAL: Rough stones covered in mud plaster to make smooth walls*

The Tower of Jericho may have been the first tower ever built. Some archaeologists think it was built to keep people safe, but no one knows for sure because it's so very, very old. The tower was connected to a thick stone wall, roughly 6 feet (2 meters) wide by 13 feet (4 meters) high. The wall and a moat surrounded a town that would eventually be called Jericho, which many people consider the oldest city in the world.

By modern standards, the tower was not very big. But it loomed high above a flat river valley. In the thousands of years since, that land started to rise slowly as new buildings were constructed. Eventually the Tower of Jericho was buried. It remained underground for a long time, until it was uncovered by archaeologists in the 1950s.

No One Knows Why

Some experts believe it was designed as a high watchtower to guard against invaders. Others argue the builders were more concerned about the nearby

Jordan River flooding, and both the wall and the moat helped reduce that risk. Ran Barkai and Roy Liran, archaeologists at Tel Aviv University, believe the tower was used for a different purpose altogether. They argue it was a giant tool to help farmers calculate the summer solstice. They discovered that the tower was built facing a nearby mountain, and the sun cast a shadow straight through its lower entryway on the longest day of the year. That's important information for farmers who needed to know when to plant their crops. It is possible the tower was built to do all these things. Whatever the reason, Barkai and Liran say the Tower of Jericho "was very much the super-skyscraper of its day."

The ancient watchtower once looked over the Jordan River Valley, but the remains are now below ground level.
GEOTHEA/SHUTTERSTOCK.COM

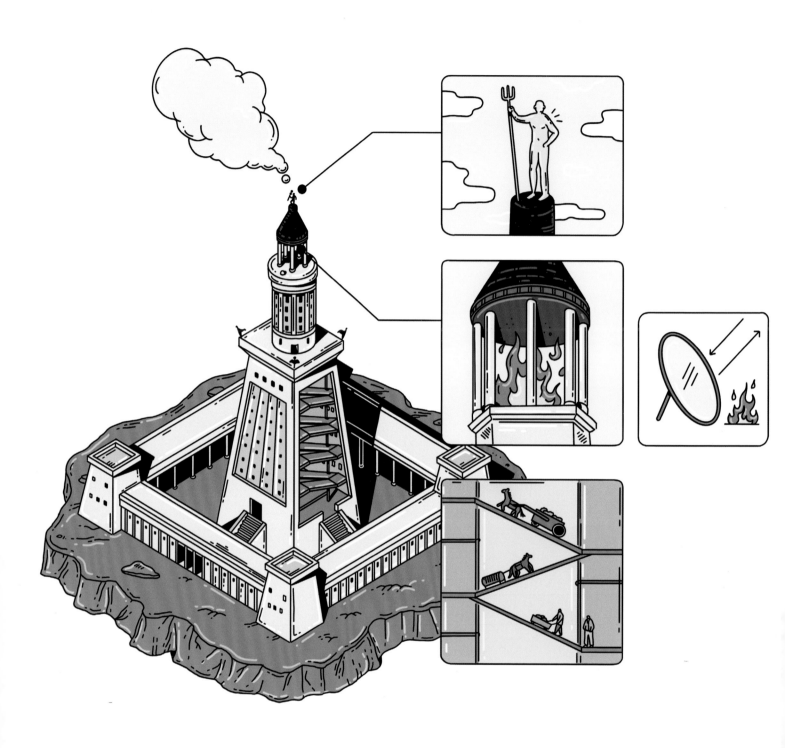

THE LIGHTHOUSE OF ALEXANDRIA

- HEIGHT: Between 338 feet (103 meters) and 387 feet (118 meters)
- YEAR FINISHED: Around 280 BCE
- DESTROYED: 1480 CE, by an earthquake
- LOCATION: Alexandria, Egypt
- ALSO KNOWN AS: Pharos of Alexandria

Eight thousand years later, a much higher tower was built on the shores of the Mediterranean Sea. The Lighthouse of Alexandria was situated on the island of Pharos, outside the harbor of the city of Alexandria, which was established by the ancient Greek king Alexander the Great.

The city was in an ideal location, at the western edge of the Nile River delta, where that mighty river enters the Mediterranean Sea. Alexandria had two natural ports, but finding the safe waters of the harbor was difficult because there were many dangerous **reefs** nearby. Ptolemy I Soter, who ruled Egypt after Alexander's death, commissioned a Greek architect and **engineer** named Sostratus of Cnidus to build a giant lighthouse. The great structure would be both a monument to the king and a guide for sailors to enter the harbor safely.

A Distant Light

At some point a furnace was built at the top of the tower so a fire could burn all night, providing a light that could be seen for miles. Later a large mirror was placed beside the furnace to reflect the fire's light even farther. Some people think the mirror was made of polished bronze and reflected sunlight in the daytime as well.

The Lighthouse of Alexandria was a stunning sight. The only human-built structure taller than it at the time was the Great Pyramid of Giza (which we will see in chapter 2). The great lighthouse was not only tall but also durable, and it remained standing for about 1,600 years! It was named one of the **Seven Wonders of the Ancient World** and became so famous that many languages adopted the word *pharos* to describe a lighthouse.

Alas, Nothing Lasts Forever

The Lighthouse of Alexandria was heavily damaged by several large earthquakes over hundreds of years. In 1480 its stones were used to build a military fortress, known as a citadel, on Pharos Island. Although the great lighthouse saved many lives, it did not keep every boat afloat. Archaeologists have discovered the remains of 40 sunken ships in the ancient harbor.

The first of the Svan towers was built more than a thousand years ago, in this region of deep gorges and snow-capped mountains. The tallest stood more than 80 feet (24 meters) above ground.
KEREN SU/GETTY IMAGES

CHÂTEAU DE COUCY

· HEIGHT: 180 feet (55 meters) · FINISHED: 1220s
· DEMOLISHED: 1917 · LOCATION: Picardy, France

Starting around the 10th century, many kings across Europe and Asia began building bigger towers and castles. Château de Coucy is generally thought to be the tallest castle ever built. It loomed over the French countryside for nearly 800 years. German soldiers occupied the medieval castle during **World War I** and dynamited it when they retreated in 1917. There is some debate about whether they did so out of anger or because they knew it might help the French follow them as they retreated.

Osaka Castle

A castle in Japan is almost as tall as Château de Coucy. The Osaka Castle is just three feet (one meter) shorter. But it's difficult to measure castles because they are often surrounded by moats and many were built on top of hills. So where would you start measuring? At the base of the tower or farther down, at the bottom of the moat or hill?

High on a Hill

Many castles were built on hilltops. One of the most famous is Edinburgh Castle, perched high on a rock right in the middle of the Scottish capital. Parts of the current castle date back to the 11th century, but archaeologists say humans have built on the site since the Iron Age.

In southern France, the Château de Montségur is perched even higher, on a clifftop that stands 557 feet (170 meters) above the nearby road. The site has been home to castles since Roman times. A fortress was built in the 13th century for members of the Cathar group, which broke away from the Roman Catholic Church. In 1243 French royal forces captured the château after a nine-month siege. Hundreds of Cathars were burned for refusing to renounce their beliefs, and the castle was destroyed. But the site was a valuable defensive position because of its views over the surrounding valleys, so another fort was built many years later. Today stone ruins are all that remain. However, there are reasons other than security to go high. Sometimes people build up because they believe in a higher power.

BUILDING BLOCKS

WINDOWS
Humans may have been making a type of glass as early as 6,000 years ago. Somewhere around 100 CE the Romans borrowed an important new technique of glassblowing from Syrian artisans who had learned to blow air into hot liquid glass before it solidified. That let the Romans make glass thinner and clearer, which led to the invention of windows. Before then, Roman buildings had holes in the wall, with shutters, to let light in.

Edinburgh Castle still stands in a commanding position above the Scottish capital, more than 900 years after it was built.
JOHN HAMILTON / EYEEM/ GETTY IMAGES

Tianning Pagoda
2007

Great Pyramid of Giza
2560 BCE

Leaning Tower of Pisa
1372

The Minaret of
Djamaâ el Djazaïr
2019

Two

SPIRITUALITY

FOR THOSE WHO DREAM OF THE HEAVENS

Buildings are physical objects made of stone, steel and other hard materials. But they can also reflect people's beliefs about what we cannot see or touch. People who believe in a god or gods have been building tall structures for thousands of years, as links between the physical and spiritual worlds.

Some of the world's oldest buildings are threatened. Experts believe the Minaret of Jam in Afghanistan could collapse. UNESCO, the United Nations Educational, Scientific and Cultural Organization, has added the tower to its List of World Heritage in Danger. The list also includes the city of Timbuktu, in Mali, which was an important trading post in the Sahara Desert for centuries. Timbuktu was also a center of Muslim teaching and is still home to the Djinguereber Mosque. And then there's the Old Walled City of Shibam in Yemen, nicknamed both the Manhattan of the Desert and the Chicago of the Desert. The 16th-century city rises from a cliff edge and includes a cluster of towers made from sun-dried mud bricks. The United Nations warns the buildings could be destroyed in the ongoing war in Yemen.

All three of the famous pyramids were built between 2550 and 2490 BCE and still stand today.
RATNAKORN PIYASIRISOROST/
GETTY IMAGES

GREAT PYRAMID OF GIZA

- *HEIGHT: 481 feet (146 meters) to tip, when finished*
- *YEAR FINISHED: Around 2560 BCE • LOCATION: Giza, Egypt*
- *YEARS AS THE WORLD'S TALLEST HUMAN-BUILT STRUCTURE: About 3,800*

One of the greatest examples of a spiritual building is the Great Pyramid of Giza in Egypt. The pyramid was not designed to be a building for people to live in. Instead, it was built as a giant tomb for the Egyptian king Pharaoh Khufu.

The pyramid was built with huge stone blocks—as many as two million! Most of the blocks were cut out of limestone with stone and copper tools. Each block weighed about 2 tons (2 metric tons), but some were as heavy as 80 tons (73 metric tons). They were measured and stacked very carefully, with only tiny gaps visible between them. The blocks created the giant stone steps we see on the outside of the pyramid today.

But How?

Modern office towers are built using giant steel cranes, diesel-powered bulldozers and cement trucks. So how did the ancient Egyptians build such a gigantic structure when work was done by hand or with the help of a donkey?

Some historians think the blocks were put into large wooden wheels and rolled up the side of the pyramid. Others suggest a ramp was used. And who did all this heavy labor? The ancient Greeks believed the Egyptians used slaves. But others think skilled craftsmen did most of the work. As with many things to do with the ancient Egyptian pyramids, no one is certain.

And Why?

The ancient Egyptians believed that the soul, or ka, remained after the body died. So the powerful pharaohs built pyramids to house their kas, along with gold, silver and fine art. After a pharaoh died, his body was wrapped with linen and preserved with embalming oils. The preserved body was called a mummy and was put in a giant coffin known as a sarcophagus. The entrance to the sarcophagus was hidden carefully to stop thieves from stealing anything inside.

PAGODAS

A pagoda is a many-tiered tower that is a sacred building erected by **Buddhists**. The word *pagoda* is used in East Asia in place of the Sanskrit word *stupa*, which refers to an earthen or **masonry** mound containing holy relics. The first stupas were built in India as places to preserve relics of the Buddha and other holy persons, in much the same way as Egyptian pyramids were built to house the remains of kings and other important people. Buddhists brought the idea of stupas from India to China in the first century CE, where the structure took on the form we now call a pagoda. Some of its features may derive from Indian temple architecture. In 611 CE, Emperor Yang of Sui had a 330-foot (100-meter)-tall wooden pagoda built in Chang'an, but it is no longer standing.

Liaodi Pagoda

Four hundred years later, during the Song dynasty, the Liaodi Pagoda was built from stone and bricks at the Kaiyuan Monastery in Dingzhou. It has 11 stories and remains the tallest brick pagoda in the world today. The Liaodi Pagoda served a number of purposes. One of them was to store important Buddhist texts brought from India by a Chinese monk. But because Dingzhou sat in a strategic location on the border between the Song and Liao dynasties, the pagoda was also used as a watchtower for soldiers looking across the border. *Liaodi* means "foreseeing the enemy's intentions."

TIANNING PAGODA

- HEIGHT: 505 feet (153 meters) to tip of spire
- YEAR FINISHED: 2007
- LOCATION: Changzhou, China

Many pagodas are very old, but the tallest pagoda in the world is one of the newest. The Tianning Pagoda is supported not by stone and brick but by 6,500 tons (5,897 metric tons) of steel. It also contains elegant details such as tropical hardwoods, jade carvings and **spires** of brass and gold. There is also a 36-ton (32.7 metric ton) bronze bell suspended near the top, which can be heard up to three miles (five kilometers) away.

Construction of the Tianning Pagoda took five years and cost $38.5 million US (300 million yuan). It took Buddhist monks more than a decade to raise the money.
ZHAOLIANG70/SHUTTERSTOCK.COM

MINARETS

Buddhists aren't the only ones who build tall towers. Muslims do too. The Islamic call to prayer, known as the adhan in Arabic, echoes from the top of minarets. These towers are attached to mosques, where Muslims worship. The crier, or muezzin, calls out five times a day for Muslims to come to the mosque to pray. Sounds that come from great heights can travel a long way, so Muslim architects started building tall minarets more than a thousand years ago. Today the call to prayer is amplified through large speakers, making it even louder.

The Minaret of Jam

In 1194 CE, high in the mountains of Afghanistan, the Minaret of Jam was built in a rugged valley where the Hari River meets the Jam River. Archaeologists believe it was built in the ancient city of Firuzkuh, the summer capital of the Ghurid dynasty. While its height was impressive, the intricate decorations,

Kufic inscriptions and turquoise tiles on the walls were stunning. The beautiful colors and designs stood in stark contrast to the drab desert surrounding the tower. The minaret inspired other architects and builders, who copied its style in India. Today the mosque and other buildings are gone, and the Minaret of Jam stands alone in a dry desert valley.

THE MINARET OF DJAMAÂ EL DJAZAÏR

- **HEIGHT:** 866 feet (264 meters) to top of tower
- **YEAR FINISHED:** 2019
- **LOCATION:** Algiers, Algeria

The call to prayer from the minaret of the Djamaâ el Djazaïr can be heard by the three million people who live in the capital city of Algeria. But that's okay—the mosque that's attached to the minaret is enormous, with enough space for 120,000 people.

HIGHLIGHTS

TOWERING TOTEMS

First Nations people of the Pacific Northwest carve and paint these iconic poles to represent their history, families and stories. The poles are usually carved out of red cedar, a soft wood that can stand in the rain for many years without rotting. The poles show humans, animals and supernatural creatures—animals such as the orca, bear, salmon, frog and raven, supernatural creatures such as the legendary Thunderbird, and stylized human faces that represent important family members. Some poles are memorials to people who have died, and some serve as pillars to support the main *beams* of a big house.

Totem poles are typically 10 to 60 feet (3 to 18 meters) in height but can be much taller. The tallest totem pole in the world is in Alert Bay, BC, at 173 feet (53 meters) high. Though totem poles and carving are an important part of First Nations culture, they were banned for many years by settler governments that attempted to forcibly assimilate Indigenous Peoples into mainstream North American culture. A new generation of carvers is again creating beautiful poles, but First Nations communities are still trying to retrieve the totem poles their people lost to museums and collectors around the world.

17

LEANING TOWER OF PISA

- **HEIGHT:** 183 feet (56 meters) to top of tower • **YEAR STARTED:** 1173
- **YEAR FINISHED:** 1372 • **TILT:** 3.97 degrees • **LOCATION:** Pisa, Italy

The spire above Ulm Minster points heavenward. It will likely remain the world's tallest church until work is finished on the Sagrada Família in Barcelona.
ALEXANDER SOROKOPUD/GETTY IMAGES

Christian churches and cathedrals too needed a way of letting people know when to gather for events like weddings and funerals. Bell towers were the end result.

The world's most famous church bell tower, or campanile, as it is called in Italian, is the Leaning Tower of Pisa. It stands behind the Pisa Cathedral and is famous for its lean. The tower started to tilt soon after construction began in the 12th century and long before it was complete. The small nine-foot (three-meter) stone foundation was made of white marble that proved too heavy for the soft soil under it. That soil was a mix of sand and clay and was softer under one side of the tower. Five years after construction started, when workers were still building the second floor, the tower began to sink on that side. But the Republic of Pisa was busy fighting wars for more than 50 years, and work was halted long enough that the ground had a chance to settle.

When construction started again, there was still a tilt to the building, but upper floors were then built with longer walls on one side to straighten the upper tower. That helped a little, but it also gave the tower a slight curve. In 1372 the bells were finally put in place near the top of the Leaning Tower of Pisa—199 years after construction started. But by the 1990s the tilt was at 5.5 degrees. Physicists said the tower could fall over at 5.44 degrees. It had to be closed for seven years to stabilize the ground under the tower, and now leans at 3.97 degrees.

Centuries in the Making

While the Leaning Tower of Pisa is the most famous church bell tower, it isn't the tallest, and the tallest part of a church isn't always the bell tower. Often it's the spire, which points up to the sky, where some Christians believe heaven is, and can be seen from a great distance. The tallest church is Ulm Minster in Germany, which took more than 500 years of building to reach its current height of 530 feet (161.5 meters)! It was started in 1377 and finished in 1890. It now stands just 3.3 feet (1 meter) higher than the former spire of the Lincoln Cathedral in England, which blew over in a windstorm more than 400 years ago.

3.97°

The Home Insurance Building
1890

The Eiffel Tower
1889

Three
INGENUITY

STRUCTURES AS INVENTIVE AS THEY ARE TALL

"FIRE!" was the front-page headline of the *Chicago Tribune* on October 11, 1871. The flames had been sparked three nights earlier in a barn next to a house. The fire spread quickly and jumped the south branch of the Chicago River before burning through the city center. "All the hotels, banks, public buildings, newspaper offices and great business blocks were swept away," the newspaper reported. When the flames were finally put out, roughly 3.3 square miles (8.5 square kilometers) of the city had been destroyed and 300 people had died. Nearly 100,000 people—one out of every three city residents—were left homeless. The Great Conflagration, as it was dubbed, left Chicago in ashes, and city leaders were determined to rebuild a new, more fire-resistant city. But that would require a lot of inventiveness, imagination and innovation.

THE HOME INSURANCE BUILDING

- *HEIGHT WHEN FINISHED: 138 feet (42 meters) in 1885 to top of building*
- *HEIGHT WITH ADDITION: 180 feet (55 meters) in 1890 to top of building*
- *LOCATION: Chicago • DEMOLISHED: 1931*

By 1883, 12 years after the fire, new office buildings were still rising in Chicago, and the Home Insurance Company hired an architect and engineer named William LeBaron Jenney to design a new tower. Jenney had worked as a railway engineer and knew a lot about steel. He started working on the Home Insurance Building in the same year the famous Brooklyn Bridge opened in New York, showing the world the kind of giant structures that could be built with steel and iron.

An Iron Skeleton

The Home Insurance Company wanted a lot of office space, so Jenney knew he needed a tall building. But the traditional method of construction, with masonry walls supporting the building, had limitations. Structures could only be so high before they would collapse under their own weight. And they would require such thick brick walls that there would be fewer windows, making the building dark (electric lighting still wasn't common). Jenney imagined a new type of structure that would be supported by a skeleton of iron beams. Iron was lighter and could carry more weight, and the frame could be clad in lighter masonry walls to make the building fireproof.

There is some debate about how Jenney came up with the idea. One of his colleagues said that Jenney noticed the strength of a birdcage one day when his wife placed a book on top of it. Some say he dreamed up the idea on a visit to the Philippines as a young man, when he saw bamboo buildings that were lightweight but still able to resist typhoons and earth-quakes.

Is It Strong Enough?

As the skeleton of the Home Insurance Building took shape, some people in Chicago began to worry it might not be strong enough. The Home Insurance Company even stopped construction to bring in a different engineer to determine whether it was safe. It was. While the first six stories were made with iron beams, the top floors had steel beams, which were being used on new bridges and proving to be stronger and more fire-resistant than iron. The Home Insurance Building was not the tallest building of its time, and it was not supported entirely by steel beams, but its design set off a building boom, and many architects and historians call it the world's first skyscraper.

At its highest, the Home Insurance Building was only 12 stories tall. But many architects and historians call it the world's first skyscraper because of its innovative iron and steel skeleton.
CHICAGO HISTORY MUSEUM, ICHI-000989; ATTRIBUTED TO J.W. TAYLOR, PHOTOGRAPHER

HIGHLIGHTS

ACCESSIBILITY IN SKYSCRAPERS

In some ways high-rises are more accessible than most shorter buildings. Taller buildings have elevators, which help people in wheelchairs move from floor to floor independently. But people living with disabilities still face barriers in tall towers. Many elevator doors don't stay open long enough. Another problem is counters that are too high for people in wheelchairs to see over.

However, some skyscrapers are now designed to be more accessible. In 2014 the CapitaGreen office tower in Singapore opened with a number of new features, such as lower counters and fewer thick posts in lobbies to help people with disabilities get around more easily. The elevator doors also stay open longer. Signs in braille on walls help people with visual impairments. And there are grab bars in washrooms and other spaces for elderly people and others who might need something stable to hold to prevent falls.

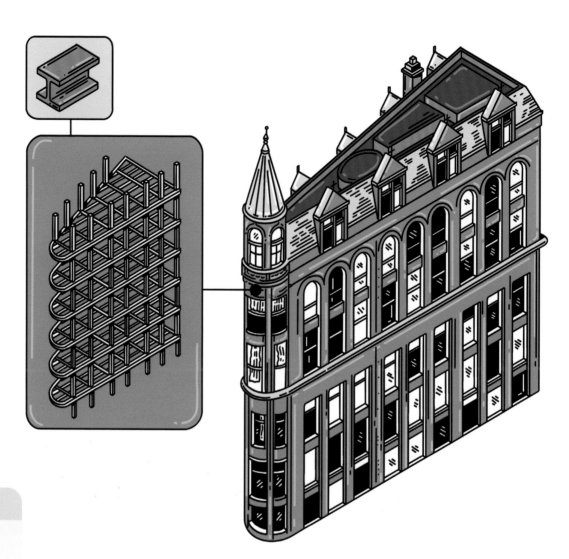

ELEVATOR
A platform or enclosure that moves up and down in a vertical shaft to move people and things. The first elevators date to the third century BCE and were called *hoists*. Heavy objects were lifted by ropes pulled by humans or animals. Modern electric elevators were invented in the 1800s, but they didn't become popular until Elisha Otis invented the modern elevator safety brake, which made it safe to travel quickly up dozens of floors on "marvelous vertical railways."

FLATIRON BUILDING

· HEIGHT: 285 feet (87 meters) to top of building · OPENED: 1902 · LOCATION: New York · FLOORS: 22

The Chicago skyline shot up after the completion of the Home Insurance Building. By 1893 the city had a dozen towers between 16 and 20 stories tall. Steel-skeleton buildings rose in other cities as well, from Boston to San Francisco. Some locals objected to the construction of such tall towers, raising concerns about increased traffic, decreased sunlight and fires far above the ground. Some cities wrote new laws to limit the height of buildings. But New York City changed its building code in 1892 to allow steel-skeleton towers, and the city started a stunning vertical rise.

In 1900 New York had more than three million people and was the largest city in the United States. Land was in high demand and very expensive. To companies with thousands of employees, building up seemed the perfect solution. In most cases that meant taller, rectangular towers. But in 1901, on an unusually shaped block, a very different tower started to rise. It was being built on a three-sided block squeezed between Broadway and Fifth Avenue. Chicago architect Daniel Burnham designed the triangular tower to fit the block perfectly. It was named the Fuller Building, after architect George Fuller. But before the unusual tower was even finished, many New Yorkers started calling it the Flatiron Building, because the triangular shape resembled the flat irons people used to press wrinkles out of their clothes.

The Bow of a Ship

Despite its great height, the building went up quickly, roughly one floor per week until it was finished. It was shaped like a right triangle, with a rounded north end measuring only six feet (two meters) across, in what the *New York Tribune* described as "an edge almost as sharp as the bow of a ship."

The Flatiron Building was not the first triangular building. A three-sided Roman temple in ancient Britain and Toronto's Gooderham Building came before it. But the Flatiron Building was much taller than the others, and that had some New Yorkers worried. Critics were concerned the building's height and its lack of a fourth side might make it fall down in especially strong winds. But the steel skeleton was designed to withstand much stronger forces than wind can produce, and it proved its strength over more than a century, weathering several hurricanes.

A Symbol of New York

New Yorkers had strong opinions about the Flatiron Building. The *New York Times* called it "a monstrosity," while writer H.G. Wells admired it for looking as though it were "ploughing up through the traffic of Broadway and Fifth Avenue in the afternoon light." Whether they loved it or hated it, New Yorkers would have to live with the Flatiron Building. Two floors were added in 1905, bringing it to its current height. Since then it's become one of the most photographed buildings in the world and is considered by many a quint-essential symbol of New York City.

More than a century after its construction stirred up controversy in New York City, the Flatiron Building is now considered an iconic landmark of the city.
TONI SHI PHOTOGRAPHY/ GETTY IMAGES

THE EIFFEL TOWER

- TOWER HEIGHT: 984 feet
  (300 meters)
- ANTENNA HEIGHT: 1,063 feet
  (324 meters) • OPENED: 1889
- LOCATION: Paris
- MATERIAL: Wrought iron

While American cities were building up, France was also dreaming up innovative new ways to scrape the sky. Gustave Eiffel was a civil engineer who made a name for himself by designing long iron railway bridges. But Eiffel would become famous for using his engineering expertise to build a bold iron-frame tower. The idea wasn't entirely new—a few mills and warehouses had been built with iron in England in the 1790s. But Eiffel believed he could design and build a much taller iron structure.

France was preparing to host the 1889 World's Fair in Paris, to commemorate the 100th anniversary of the French Revolution. Organizers also wanted to demonstrate France's industrial power, and building the world's tallest building was an eye-catching way to do that.

Though the tower would bear Gustave Eiffel's name, it was largely designed by Maurice Koechlin and Emile Nouguier, both of whom worked for Eiffel. Koechlin was a structural engineer who worked with Eiffel on the metal skeleton inside the Statue of Liberty and would later draw a plan for a tower that resembled "a great pylon, consisting of four lattice girders standing apart at the base and coming together at the top, joined together by metal trusses."

Eiffel and his team envisioned a tower that stretched up roughly the height of an 80-story office building. To support a structure that big, they knew they would need huge, sturdy foundations in the ground. They didn't want a leaning tower in Paris, like the famous tower in Pisa!

Towering Backlash

Parisians had never seen such a high building, and, like New Yorkers, they had some strong opinions about it! Some marveled at the ingenuity of the design, but others hated it. A group called Artists against the Eiffel Tower signed a petition, which they sent to the government and the influential newspaper *Le Temps*. They compared the tower to "a gigantic black smokestack, crushing under its barbaric bulk Notre Dame, the Tour Saint-Jacques, the Louvre, the Dome of les Invalides,

the Arc de Triomphe…we shall see stretching like a blot of ink the hateful shadow of the hateful column of bolted sheet metal."

Some opponents changed their minds as the tower was built and grew to love it. The Eiffel Tower was the world's tallest for more than four decades, an impressive record for something that was originally supposed to be temporary and was scheduled to be torn down in 1909. It remains an international symbol of France and one of the most popular tourist destinations in the world.

Big Ben
1859

Empire State Building
1931

CN Tower
1976

Four

UTILITY

SOMETIMES BEING THE TALLEST THING AROUND IS USEFUL

Tall towers often attract a lot of attention because of their height and striking appearance, but many were built to be useful. Big Ben is probably the most famous clock tower in the world, and though it is a beautifully crafted structure, it has performed a very practical purpose for 160 years—it's told millions of people what time it is.

BIG BEN

- HEIGHT: 315 feet (96 meters) to tip
- COMPLETED: 1859
- LOCATION: London, England
- FLOORS: 11

Big Ben is not the tower's official name. Its formal name is the Elizabeth Tower. But most people use the nickname of the giant bell that hangs in the tower, which is Big Ben. It wasn't the first clock tower to stand in that spot. Various clocks or sundials have stood there since 1290. When a fire destroyed most of Westminster Palace in the 1830s, a competition was held to design a new palace and tower. It would take more than 15 years before the clock started keeping time. An architect named Sir Charles Barry won the competition to build the palace, and construction started on the tower. It was helped along by the fact that the building site was so close to the River Thames. Materials like iron girders, bricks and granite could be barged there relatively easily.

Telling Time

Barry's design did not feature a clock, so *another* competition was held, in 1846, to find a clockmaker. The judge had high standards and specified that the clock had to strike the bell every hour within one second of the real time. He also wanted the time telegraphed twice a day to the Royal Observatory Greenwich. Those high standards meant it would take another seven years to build a suitable clock.

A Revolutionary Mechanism

While tower construction continued, an amateur clockmaker named Edmund Beckett Denison developed what became known as the "double three-legged gravity escapement." The invention helped the

clock keep accurate time by making sure the swinging pendulum was not slowed down by the wind. It was so reliable that clocks around the world were built with the same mechanism.

A Crack and Other Delays

The giant bell for the tower was placed on a carriage pulled by 16 white horses and trotted across Westminster Bridge. Despite the bell's grand arrival, a crack soon appeared when it was first tested. So a lighter bell had to be cast. When the tower was finally finished, and the clock installed, there was—you guessed it—another delay! This time the cast-iron clock hands were too heavy to move and had to be replaced by lighter copper hands. There were even more delays to come, including another serious crack in the Great Bell that had to be fixed. Since 1863 Big Ben has marked the passage of time with only a few interruptions.

Bombs and Broadcasts

The British Broadcasting Corporation first broadcast Big Ben's chimes on the radio on New Year's Eve in 1923. During World War II the clock was unlit so German bomber pilots couldn't see it. In 1941 a bomb hit the top of the clock tower but failed to destroy it. The clock has been stopped a handful of times for repair, and on New Year's Eve 1962 heavy snow and ice caused Big Ben to ring in the new year 10 minutes late.

Big Ben catches the eye, even at night. Its striking neo-Gothic style and accurate four-faced chiming clock have helped millions of people keep track of the time.
ULTRAFORMA/GETTY IMAGES

HIGHLIGHTS

SO WHO WAS BEN?

The first theory is that the name comes from Sir Benjamin Hall, the First Commissioner of Works in London. This seems the most likely explanation, as his name was inscribed on the bell. But there is another theory that it was named after Ben Caunt, a champion heavyweight boxer of the time.

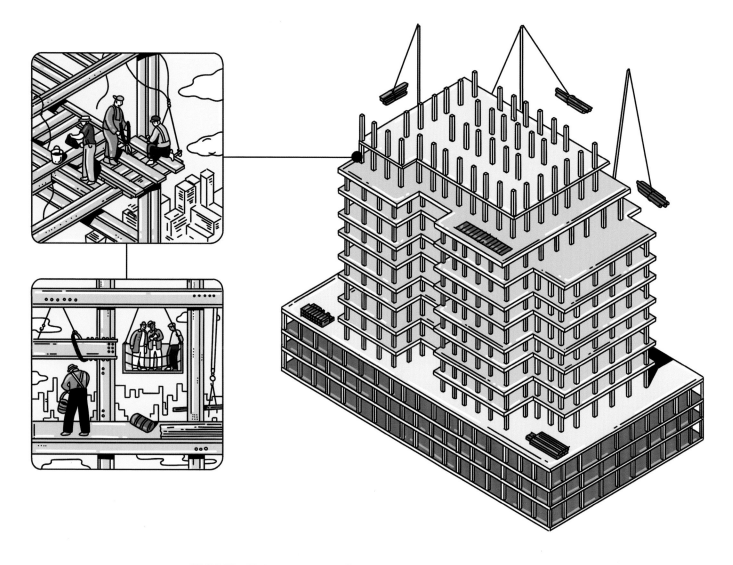

THE EMPIRE STATE BUILDING

- BUILDING HEIGHT: 1,250 feet (381 meters) · ANTENNA TIP: 1,454 feet (443 meters)
- OPENED: 1931 · LOCATION: New York · FLOORS: 102

Big Ben stood head and shoulders above the London horizon for decades. But in New York City, the skyline had been constantly changing, as ever taller buildings sprung up. By 1930 builders were competing to build the tallest tower in the world. A group of investors announced they would build a colossal tower called the Empire State Building. Construction started before the design was finalized, and the owners soon realized they needed to make it more useful than the buildings around it. They had paid a lot for the land,

which was home to half of the famous Waldorf Astoria Hotel, and they would have to make their money back. That meant they needed a really tall building that would hold a lot of people. At first they imagined a 50- or 60-story tower, but they soon decided it should be even taller.

Great Location, Terrible Timing

The building was close to subway and train stations, so lots of workers could get there easily. While its location was good, the timing of its construction was terrible.

The New York Stock Exchange crashed on October 24, 1929. This was the start of the **Great Depression**, a period in which millions of people lost their jobs. All of a sudden, few businesses wanted to rent office space.

Instead of canceling the Empire State Building project, the owners made it bigger, buying even more land and making its foundations even wider. They added another 16 floors on top, in the shape of a high metal crown the owners said would be used as a mooring mast for dirigibles. They imagined thousands of people traveling in such airships in the future and hoped a mooring mast would be useful.

A Firm Foundation

Once the existing hotel was demolished, and the enormous concrete foundation poured, work began on the building itself. Like the Flatiron Building, the Empire State Building had a steel skeleton, and for such a massive structure, it went up quickly—at the dizzying speed of more than four floors per week. As the steel rose higher, brick-layers and other workers filled in the frame-work with 10 million bricks, hundreds of tons of aluminum and stainless steel, and 200,000 cubic feet (5,663 cubic meters) of limestone and granite.

A Construction Army

Thousands of workers built the Empire State Building. On one especially busy day, more than 3,400 people worked on it. Temporary cafés and food stands were set up on unfinished floors to feed the crews so they wouldn't need to leave the site. It was good work at a time when jobs were hard to find. But it was also dangerous. Steelworkers spent hours perched on the edge of steel beams, dangling hundreds of feet above the city. The *Saturday Evening Post* spoke to a construction foreman who said workers could "find themselves on a narrow beam with no handhold, fall flat on their stomach, clutch the beam, wrap themselves round it, shut their eyes and gasp as though drowning." By the time the building was finished, at least five construction workers had died on the job.

Opening Day

The Empire State Building officially opened on May 1, 1931, 18 months after construction started. The top 16 stories were capped by an **art deco** spire, with observatories on the 86th and 102nd floors. The Empire State Building was an architectural success, winning a gold medal for excellence. But it risked being a financial failure because so much office space was empty.

The Empire State Building is no longer the tallest building in New York City. The 104-floor One World Trade Center (to the right of the Empire State Building in the distance) was opened in 2013.
MATTEO COLOMBO/GETTY IMAGES

The observatory helped. It was the highest place in New York and attracted visitors from all over. Advertisements appeared in newspapers and on the backs of train tickets. In its first year, a million people paid a dollar each to enjoy the breathtaking view and spent more money to buy food and drinks. The observatories soon made as much money as rent from office space.

Observatories a Boom, Mooring Mast a Bust

The mooring mast wasn't practical—in fact, it was dangerous. Strong winds and updrafts made it difficult to navigate a giant airship to the top of the building, and the spires of other buildings were a safety hazard. As if that weren't enough, passengers would have to walk out along a narrow ramp roughly 106 stories above the ground! The idea was destined to

fail—only one airship ever tied up to the Empire State Building's mast, and it had to circle the building 25 times in strong winds first. The crew had to leave a few minutes later, when a strong gust of wind rocked the airship.

Sky-High Radio

If the Empire State Building's height couldn't be used for airships, it could be used for radio stations. The NBC network leased office space on the 85th floor and transmitted AM radio from an antenna on the roof. NBC even sent its first experimental television and FM radio signals from there. Before long the building was home to various radio and TV stations, which paid the owners a lot of rent. By 1950 there were so many that a dedicated 217-foot (66-meter) television tower was added.

Using the Empire State Building as a mooring mast for airships was not practical, but the building's height has been an excellent location for broadcast antennas.
NEIL EMMERSON/GETTY IMAGES

THE CN TOWER

- HEIGHT: 1,815 feet (553 meters) to tip
- OPENED: 1976
- LOCATION: Toronto

New York wasn't the only city with radio and television stations needing tall transmitters. In booming Toronto, where more tall buildings were being built, residents began complaining about poor television reception. In those days, most television shows were broadcast through the airwaves rather than through cables. The old transmission towers in Toronto were no longer tall enough to send clear signals to all televisions in the area, so a taller tower was needed.

In 1973 the Canadian National Railway started construction on the CN Tower. When it opened in 1976, the top of the antenna spire was 42 feet (13 meters) higher than the Ostankino Tower's in Moscow. That tower too was constructed to transmit television and radio signals. Construction began on it in 1963, and when the building was finished in 1967, its antenna soared 1,771 feet (540 meters), eclipsing the Empire State Building.

The designers of the CN Tower certainly took pride in its being the world's tallest, and we'll talk more about building just for bragging rights in the next chapter.

BUILDING BLOCKS

BOLTS AND RIVETS
A bolt is a long metal object that screws into a metal nut and fastens two things together, such as an upright *column* to a vertical beam. A rivet is a short, smooth piece of metal that holds two larger pieces of metal together. Before it's installed, a rivet has a wide head on one end. Once it's fed through the hole in each piece of metal, the narrow end is pounded to make it wide as well. Rivets replaced bolts on many buildings because they are shorter and do not loosen when the building vibrates.

Chrysler Building
1930

Asinelli Tower
(Torre degli Asinelli)
1119

Burj Khalifa
2010

Five

RIVALRY

COMPETITION TO BUILD SKY-HIGH

Some of the world's tallest buildings are tall simply because their builders wanted to beat everyone else. The best example of how rivalry propelled builders upward is the so-called Race into the Sky, as New York newspapers dubbed a competition between two buildings in 1929. It was a race between millionaires and architects to claim the title of world's tallest building.

CHRYSLER BUILDING

- *HEIGHT TO TIP: 1,046 feet (319 meters)*
- *TOP FLOOR: 899 feet (274 meters)*
- *OPENED TO PUBLIC: May 27, 1930*
- *LOCATION: New York*

Architects William Van Alen and H. Craig Severance were former business partners who became rivals after they split up. Van Alen was hired by Walter Chrysler, the founder of the Chrysler car company, to build a bold new skyscraper that would

bear his name. Chrysler was willing to spend millions on the skyscraper and declared it would be a "monument to me." Van Alen hoped the Chrysler Building would be the tallest in the world and would look unlike anything ever built. He changed the design several times, sharing the details with Walter Chrysler, who would unroll the paper plans on the floor and inspect them carefully. Though their plans were still changing, they announced to the world in 1928 that they would build a new tower that would be 820 feet (250 meters) high.

40 Wall Street

A month later the Manhattan Company bank announced it would build a giant new office tower at 40 Wall Street, a 20-minute subway ride from where the Chrysler Building would rise. H. Craig Severance, also an investor, would design the skyscraper. Prime New York real estate was expensive, so the company decided the only way to make money was to build up—way up—and make its building 20 feet higher than the Chrysler Building. It also wanted the tower to be built quickly in order to save money. Other New York skyscrapers had taken two years to build. The Manhattan Company wanted its building to rise in just one.

Rivals Race

Construction started on both buildings, and by the summer of 1929 the newspapers were following the competition closely. Both architects changed their plans many times during construction and kept them closely guarded secrets. Van Alen altered the top of his tower, stretching what was once a short cap into a multi-*arched* stainless steel dome, with triangular windows to make the building look as though it were rocketing up into the sky. But the architect kept his crowning achievement a secret until the day it was installed.

A Surprise Ending

Once Van Alen was confident his rival's building was nearly finished, he decided to unveil his crowning achievement. On October 23 he stood a few blocks away from the Chrysler Tower, watching the top of his creation with dread. He squinted as a crane lifted a gigantic, gleaming spire from the inside of the building and perched it on top. The spire, or vertex, weighed nearly 54,000 pounds (24,500 kilograms) and was 185 feet (56 meters) high. The vertex had been winched to the top floor of the building in five separate pieces, in secret, and assembled there. Now, as the crane lifted the vertex, Van Alen was worried something might go terribly wrong, like a gust of wind blowing the spire over and sending it crashing down onto the street. He was also concerned that the crane, positioned on a wooden platform 860 feet (260 meters) in the air, wasn't big enough to lift the heavy vertex.

These days such a move might not be allowed for safety reasons, but it went ahead because regulations were not as strict in 1929. Van Alen held his breath and watched the spire rise "like a butterfly emerging from a cocoon," as he later described it. It was hoisted into place and then steelworkers riveted it to the building. The crowning of the Chrysler Building took just 90 minutes, with no fanfare or ceremony. The bold new tower was suddenly the world's tallest. William Van Alen had beaten his old friend in the Race into the Sky.

A Short and Contentious Reign

Standing on the sidewalk, it was difficult for anyone to see which building was taller, and it was a month before the news became official. When it did, some of the architects working with H. Craig Severance complained that their competitor hadn't really won. They said the observation deck on their building was higher than the top floor of the Chrysler Building. Only the spire made the difference. It didn't matter for long— 11 months later the Empire State Building beat them both.

The dome on the Chrysler Building is still an eye-catching feature of the New York skyline more than 90 years after it was built.
BY DREA DIZON/GETTY IMAGES

WOMEN WHO DREAM HIGH

For a long time, most architects were men. Natalie de Blois was one of the early pioneers who started to change that. Working with the firm Skidmore, Owings & Merrill, she played a key role in the design of several skyscrapers. But the men she worked with got most of the credit. "These were celebrated buildings that the press fawned over, but Natalie's name was never mentioned," fellow architect Beverly Willis told the *New York Times*. De Blois's tallest building was the 52-floor Union Carbide headquarters, which was built in the late 1950s.

It took many decades for Natalie de Blois to receive the attention she deserved, and even then it was only for some of her work. But she set a precedent for other women in architecture. Architect Jeanne Gang in Chicago has designed several tall buildings, including the 101-story St. Regis Chicago, which was completed in 2020. And women took the lead in designing Africa's tallest building, the 55-story Leonardo in Johannesburg, which was finished in 2019. "I really had to work hard to prove myself," architect Malika Walele said in an interview with CNN. "I really had to step up and speak out—make sure that I was being heard by the men."

ASINELLI TOWER (TORRE DEGLI ASINELLI)

- *HEIGHT TODAY: 319 feet (97.2 meters) to top of building*
- *HEIGHT WHEN FINISHED: about 229 feet (70 meters)*
- *FINISHED: 1119*
- *LOCATION: Bologna, Italy*

Long before Manhattan's Race into the Sky, a medieval version of the vertical rivalry took place in Italy. Bologna was a busy place in the Middle Ages, with rich merchants boasting their wealth in brick and stone. The most eye-catching way to do this was to build tall towers. At its peak Bologna had more than 100. Only a fraction of them remain today.

But two at the entrance to the old city now stand as a famous visual symbol of both the city and architectural rivalry. The Two Towers of Bologna—Le Due Torri, in Italian—were built just a stone's throw from each other in the early 1100s. The taller one is called the Asinelli and is now the tallest leaning medieval tower in the world. Yes, it's leaning, like the famous Leaning Tower of Pisa. But neither it nor the Pisa leans as much as the Garisenda Tower, which has a tilt that can make pedestrians think it's falling over when clouds move above it.

The Two Towers

Asinelli and Garisenda were built by wealthy families who competed for money and prestige. The Asinelli Tower was started in 1109 and completed in 1119. It was paid for by Gherardo Asinelli. The Garisenda was started a few years later by Filippo and Oddo Garisendi, brothers who may have been jealous of the Asinellis' tower. Bologna's towers kept their wealthy occupants safe and let local soldiers watch for enemies. This was a serious concern at a time when the city was deeply divided between the Guelphs, who supported the Pope, and the Ghibellines, who supported the Holy Roman Emperor.

It takes only a quick glance to see which of the Two Towers won. The Asinelli Tower is much taller, and tourists can still climb 498 steps to take in its magnificent views. The Garisenda is now only 157 feet (48 meters) high. By the 13th century it was leaning so precipitously that the top 39 feet (12 meters) had to be removed.

The Two Towers of Bologna, believed to be more than 900 years old, are still standing.
FRANCESCO RICCARDO IACOMINO/GETTY IMAGES

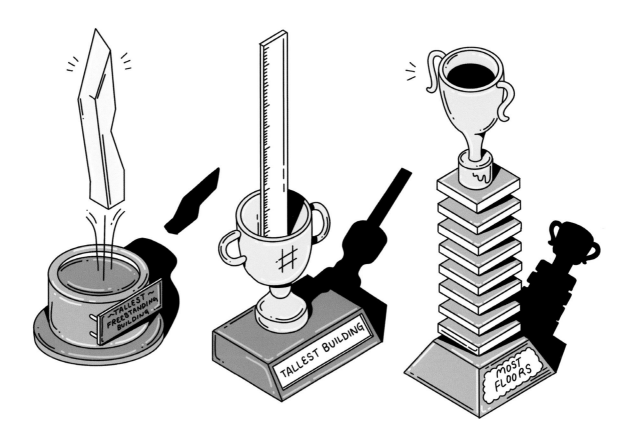

BUILDING BLOCKS

WHO'S NEXT?
In 2016 developers in Dubai announced plans for a new tower, based on the mythical Hanging Gardens of Babylon, that would be "a notch" taller than the Burj Khalifa. And Saudi Arabia is building a tower in the port city of Jeddah that promises to be the world's first building to reach 3,281 feet (1,000 meters). But work on Jeddah Tower stalled in 2018 with less than a quarter of the building finished. As I write, it still isn't finished. But if history is anything to go by, we may soon see a tower that's taller than the Burj Khalifa.

BURJ KHALIFA

HEIGHT: *2,722 feet (830 meters) to tip*
OPENED: *2010*
LOCATION: *Dubai*
FLOORS: *163*

Rivalries have been going on as long as people have been building, and there's no reason to think they'll stop. Just look at the world's tallest tower now and some of the plans already in the works to beat it.

When the Burj Khalifa was finished, the stunning skyscraper towered over everything in the city of Dubai. It broke a long list of world records: tallest building, tallest freestanding structure, most floors, highest occupied floor, highest outdoor observation deck, elevator with the longest travel distance, and tallest service elevator. The tip of the tower is nearly twice the height of the Empire State Building!

It isn't surprising that the world's tallest building was built in Dubai. The government there decided a long time ago to turn itself into a global financial center, with world-class office towers. It might seem impossible to imagine a building taller than the Burj Khalifa. But, of course, people are competitive, and that's exactly what some of them hope to build.

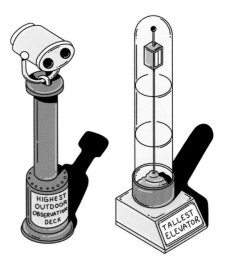

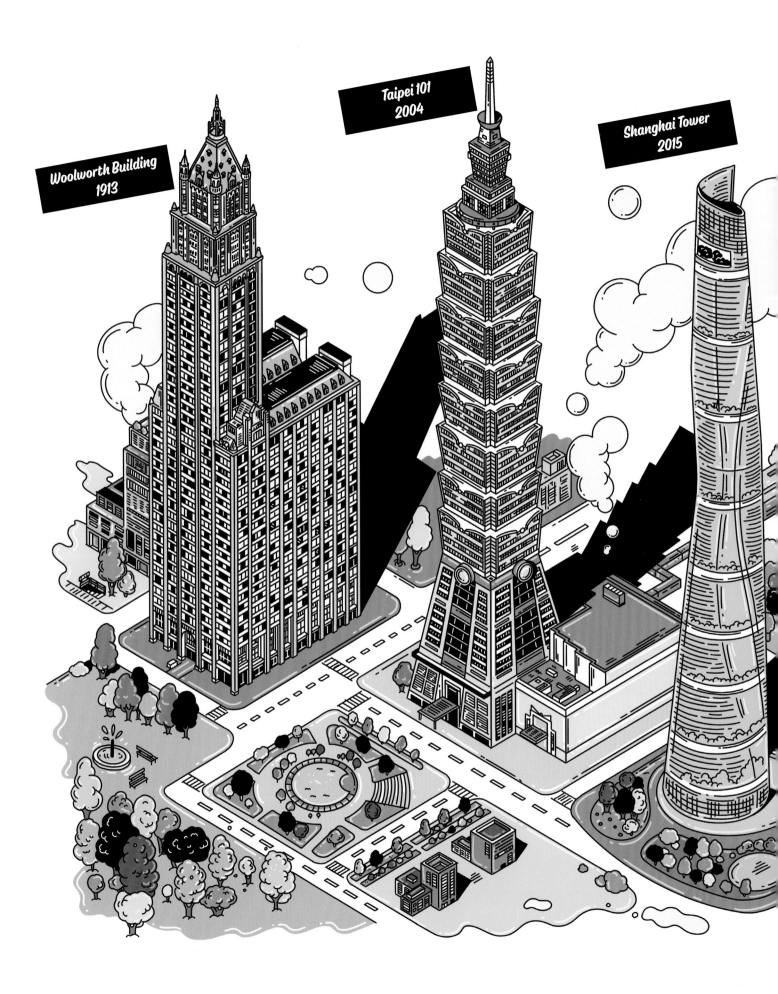

Woolworth Building
1913

Taipei 101
2004

Shanghai Tower
2015

Six

BEAUTY

BUILT TO BE BEAUTIFUL

When New York millionaires and architects first dreamed of constructing the world's tallest building in the 1920s, they had one landmark to beat—the Woolworth Building. It was the tallest in the world at the time. Many of the people who walked past it or who stepped inside the elegant lobby said it was also one of the most beautiful, looking more like a cathedral or museum than an office building.

WOOLWORTH BUILDING

- *HEIGHT: 792 feet (241 meters) to tip*
- *OPENED: 1913*
- *LOCATION: New York*
- *FLOORS: 55*

The building was the dream of Frank Winfield Woolworth, who had become a millionaire by selling small items for a nickel or a dime in hundreds of stores across the United States, Canada and Great Britain. He decided to spare no expense in building the world's tallest tower. Woolworth hired architect Cass Gilbert, who had already made a name for himself designing buildings that combined classical European and modern North American styles. "I do not want a mere building," he said. "I want something that will be an ornament to the city." Woolworth had visited Europe and grown to love the grand architecture, like the **Gothic** Houses of Parliament in London, Big Ben, the Paris Opera House and many grand cathedrals.

A Mix of Old and New

Gilbert first designed a building that would be 420 feet (130 meters) high. But the height was soon increased. And while the height was certainly impressive, the style was stunning. Gilbert's design combined Italian, French and modern

Renaissance styles. The building was constructed around a modern steel frame, but the exterior walls looked like the older European buildings he admired. The lower walls were clad in limestone, while the higher ones were covered in beautiful cream-colored terra-cotta panels that were also fireproof. The panels included thousands of detailed sculptures, around thousands of windows.

The building was designed before air conditioners were introduced, so windows were needed to keep the offices cool in the summer. Around the windows were bright blue paintings with gold tracings. The tower was topped by a copper pyramid and surrounded by spires. Its striking silhouette, which Gilbert described as "light, graceful, delicate and flame-like," could be seen for miles. Down on the sidewalk, visitors walked past outside walls that evoked old Gothic churches, before passing under the large arched windows at the main entrance and proceeding into a luxurious lobby.

BUILDING BLOCKS

EXPRESS ELEVATORS AND SKY LOBBIES

Express elevators don't stop at all floors. Some stop on just the upper floors of the building. Others stop only at a floor called a *sky lobby*, which has another series of elevators that carries people to upper floors. Express elevators and sky lobbies are ideal for taller buildings because they reduce the number of elevators needed and the number of floors people will have to stop at on their way up.

The Woolworth Building stood as the world's tallest building from 1913 to 1930. It was also praised for its elegant design and called the "Cathedral of Commerce."
BIGAPPOLIS/TOM RIDINGER/GETTY IMAGES

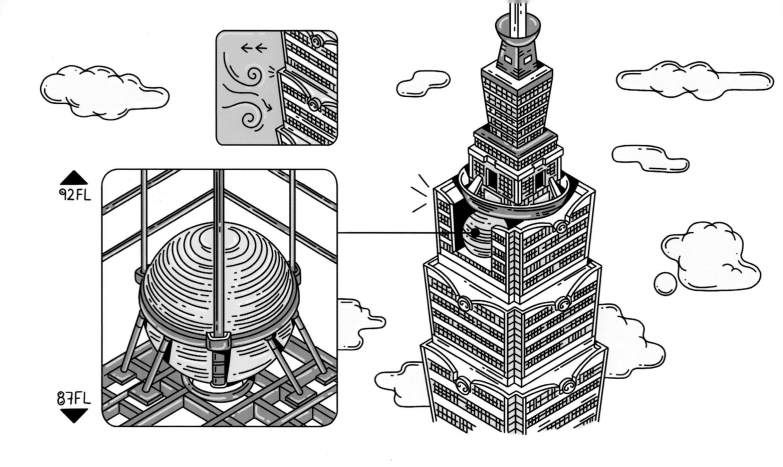

92FL

87FL

TAIPEI 101

- HEIGHT: 1,671 feet (509 meters) to tip
- OPENED: 2004
- LOCATION: Taipei, Taiwan
- FLOORS: 101

Ninety years after the Cathedral of Commerce rose over New York, another skyscraper influenced by beautiful religious design was built on the other side of the world. Taipei 101 was the world's tallest inhabited building when it opened. It has modern environmental features, including rainwater collection and double-paned windows to block UV light and lower cooling costs. (We'll find out more about how today's tall buildings are shrinking their *environmental footprint* in the final chapter.)

Innovative and Beautiful

For all its innovation, what catches the eye of millions of people who look at Taipei 101 is its beautiful shape. Architects C.Y. Lee and C.P. Wang modeled their supertall tower on a traditional Chinese pagoda, with the main tower separated into eight stacking levels, called dou, each of which is eight stories high. The number eight is lucky in Chinese culture and is associated with abundance and good fortune. The architects followed the principles of feng shui, an ancient Chinese practice based on creating balance between people and the environment. They said the building's eight dou give it a sense of rhythm and scale that "diminishes its height through repeated order."

While many Western skyscrapers either shoot straight up or slope inward like a pyramid, the eight levels of Taipei 101 flare up and out, reflecting traditional Chinese values of welcoming the natural world. The building also includes many square and round shapes, to balance the yin and yang of the building. In designing Taipei 101, architects C.Y. Lee and C.P. Wang struck a balance between old and new.

SHANGHAI TOWER

- *HEIGHT: 2,073 feet (632 meters) to tip*
- *COMPLETED: 2015*
- *LOCATION: Shanghai*
- *FLOORS: 128*

Eleven years after Taipei 101 was finished, a new skyscraper rose over China's financial hub and biggest city. The Shanghai Tower is the tallest building in China and was the third of three skyscrapers that went up in Shanghai's new Lujiazui Finance and Trade Zone. The building has a curved facade like a spiral, which makes it look like it's twisting as it stretches up into the sky. The shape was highly unusual when it was built in 2008 and is a striking visual symbol of China's recent growth into an economic powerhouse. But it is the tower's beauty that catches the world's attention.

Top of Its Class

The Shanghai Tower won the annual Emporis Skyscraper Award in 2016 for its "elegant spiraling cylindrical shape" and other features. But beauty isn't everything, and sometimes it's not practical. The building's unusual shape left less space for desks and office equipment than in a rectangular building. This meant tenants would be paying money for unusable space, and for the first few years after the tower was built, many floors stayed empty. The impracticality of the shape hasn't stopped others from building twisting towers. Since 2010 more than two dozen have risen. While beauty may be impractical sometimes, it's still popular. However, some tall structures are *not* designed to be popular or beautiful but are built for a specific reason—to get dirty jobs done.

The Shanghai World Financial Center, with a large trapezoid-shaped opening near the top, stands on the left. The curved glass walls of the Shanghai Tower rise above it on the right.
CHENGGANG CAI/GETTY IMAGES

The INCO Superstack
1972

NASA Vehicle
Assembly Building
1966

Seven

INDUSTRY

RISING UP TO GET THE JOB DONE

While some of the world's tallest structures are loved and called beautiful, others are loathed and called ugly. One of the most hated types of tower is the smokestack. These giant chimneys rise high above industrial buildings such as factories, power plants and smelters. Although they're not popular, smokestacks serve an important purpose—they lift noxious gases like carbon dioxide, sulfur dioxide and nitrogen oxide up and away from the people who live and work nearby. Large industrial chimneys may also act as drafts, drawing fresh air down to help stoke the fire at the bottom. Some of these chimney stacks are as tall as modern skyscrapers.

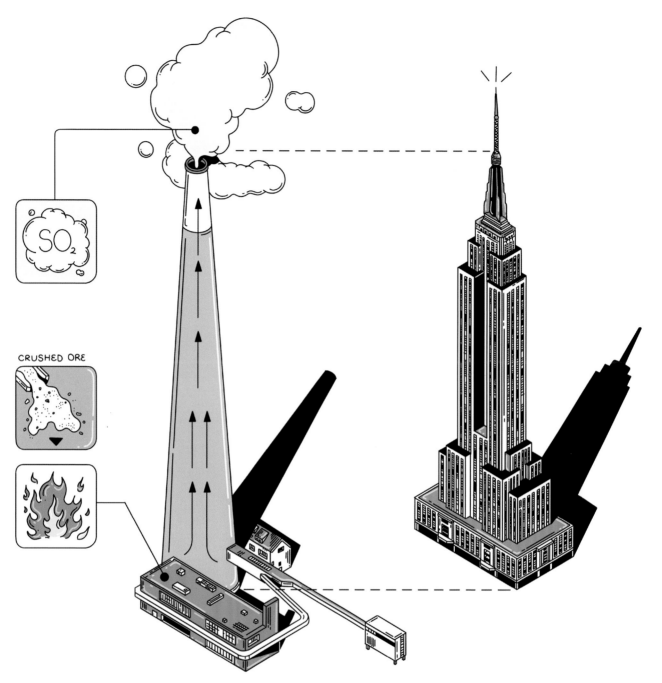

CRUSHED ORE

SO$_2$

THE INCO SUPERSTACK

· *HEIGHT: 1,250 feet (381 meters) top of stack*
· *OPENED: 1972* · *LOCATION: Sudbury, Ontario*

MARK VISOSKY

Chimneys have been around for centuries, but they got much taller during the Industrial Revolution in the 1700s. At first chimneys were built into the walls of factory furnaces where coal or wood was burned to power steam engines. The furnace needed fresh air to keep its fire burning and an escape for the smoke it created. A chimney stack helped with both. As industrial cities like Manchester and Pittsburgh became crowded with factories, chimney stacks rose above them like smoky forests of brick trees. The rise of smokestacks stalled for a while in the early 1900s, when factories started using mechanical fans to suck in air and switched to diesel engines and electric motors, which produced less smoke. But coal-fired power plants and smelters kept belching out smoke, some of them so much that separate stand-alone chimney stacks were built beside them. At around the same time, tough new laws were introduced that required even taller chimneys.

Breaking Records

The city of Sudbury is built on the rocky outcrops of the Canadian Shield, where huge deposits of nickel, copper, platinum, palladium and other metals lie under lakes and forests. Mining started in the region in the 1880s. By the 1930s Sudbury had some of the world's tallest stacks, including two chimneys that were 492 feet (150 meters) high. But they weren't high enough to move all the pollution from the smelters away from the city. The International Nickel Company, INCO, was the world's largest nickel-mining and -smelting operation in the world, and in 1970 it started work on the world's tallest chimney stack at that time. When it was finished, the INCO Superstack was the same height as the Empire State Building's roof and was briefly the tallest free-standing structure in Canada.

Most of the time, the giant steel-reinforced concrete stack did what it was supposed to do: it lifted the noxious gases up into the prevailing winds, which blew the pollution far away. But when there was a *temperature inversion*, and the air high above Sudbury was warmer than the air down in the city, the pollution was forced back to the ground. Even when the winds were cooperating, the pollution became a problem over a larger area. Sulfur dioxide spread as far as 150 miles (241 kilometers) from the INCO Superstack.

A Cleaner Future?

The mine's owners spent more than a billion dollars on new technologies for capturing more pollution. They built a cleaning plant that reduced sulfur dioxide emissions by 85 percent and another small plant, called a baghouse, that reduced metal particulates. There was a lot less smoke as a result, so they decided to build two smaller chimneys to replace the giant superstack that had loomed on the Sudbury skyline for half a century.

In 2020 the Vale mining company, which bought INCO, started dismantling the giant structure. While some old smokestacks have been demolished over the years, that couldn't happen in Sudbury. The INCO Superstack had hazardous material inside and would have to be taken apart carefully—especially since the closest house was less than 650 feet (198 meters) from the base of the giant chimney. The company announced it would take the stack apart piece by piece, recycling steel and other useful materials along the way.

The INCO Superstack stood for decades as one of the tallest human-built structures on Earth. But, like the great Lighthouse of Alexandria and many other towers built in the past, it did not remain standing—a reminder that nothing built by humans lasts forever.

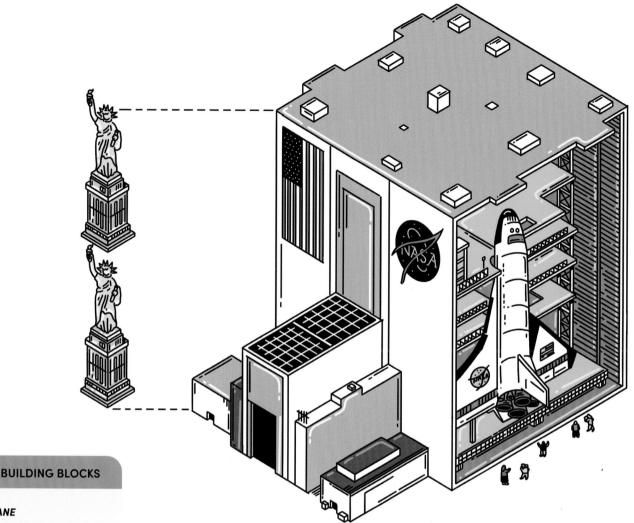

THE CRANE

This tall machine is used to move heavy objects by lifting them from an arm or beam. The first cranes may have been used in Mesopotamia around 2000 BCE to lift water for irrigation in farming. The ancient Greeks added winches and pulleys to cranes and used them for building stone temples. The Romans used cranes to lift huge stone blocks into place high on buildings. Nowadays thin tower cranes rise with skyscrapers, balancing two long arms over a steel mast. One of the arms balances the crane, the other has a cable and hook that lifts heavy materials up onto buildings. Three tower cranes worked on the Burj Khalifa, often 24 hours a day.

NASA VEHICLE ASSEMBLY BUILDING

- HEIGHT: 525 feet (160 meters) to top of building
- LENGTH AND WIDTH: 716 feet (218 meters) by 518 feet (158 meters)
- FINISHED: 1966
- LOCATION: Titusville, Florida

Smokestacks aren't the only tall industrial structures. The Vehicle Assembly Building at NASA's Kennedy Space Center in Florida is one of the largest buildings in the world—nearly twice the height of the Statue of Liberty. It is the tallest single-floor building in the world and the tallest building in the United States that is not in a city. It was built in the 1960s to provide a covered space in which to assemble large prebuilt components of space vehicles, like the *Saturn V* rocket and the space shuttles. The building has huge doors—the world's largest—to let those space vehicles in and out. All four doors are 456 feet (139 meters) high and are so big it takes 45 minutes to open or close them all the way. The building also has five gigantic cranes to lift space equipment. Almost everything about the Vehicle Assembly Building is large—even the American flag on the outside wall is the world's largest, at 209 feet (64 meters) long by 110 feet (33.5 meters) wide.

The Vehicle Assembly Building has proved itself useful for more than half a century, allowing engineers to put rocket pieces together indoors. But we will see in the next chapter that other tall buildings go up just to let people get a better view of what's outside.

The NASA Vehicle Assembly Building is so big it can generate its own weather. On especially humid days, rain clouds can form inside the building. Giant air conditioners are used to control the moisture.
MEINZAHN/GETTY IMAGES

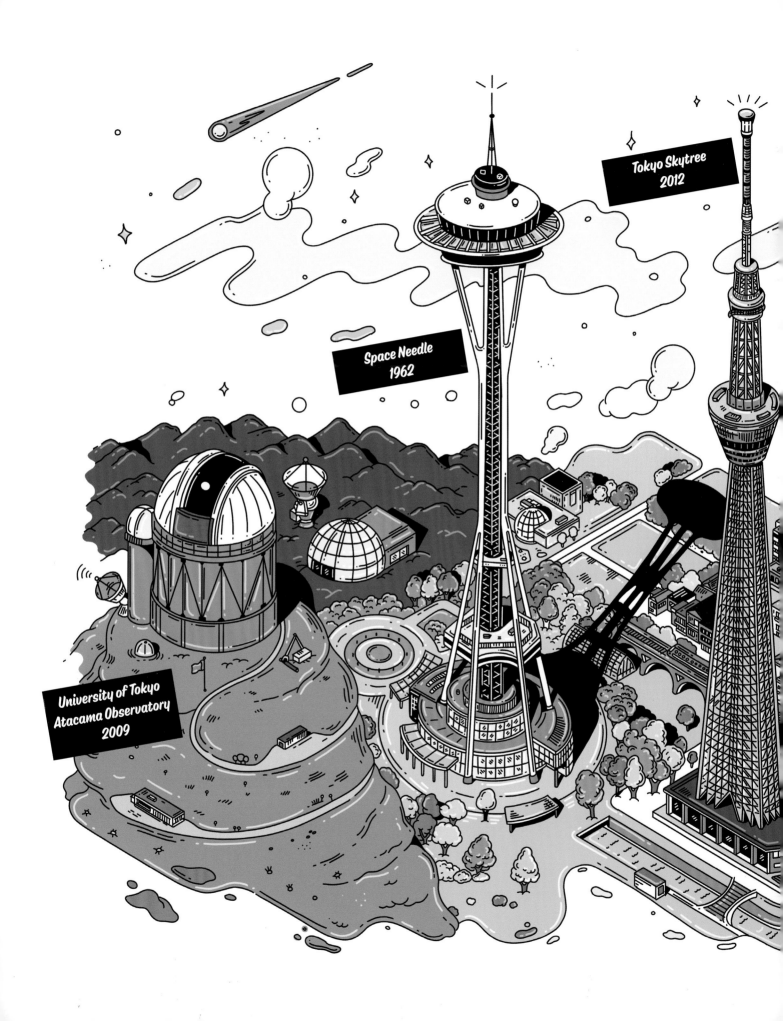

Tokyo Skytree
2012

Space Needle
1962

University of Tokyo
Atacama Observatory
2009

Eight
OBSERVATORIES

BUILDING A BIRD'S-EYE VIEW

Sometimes tall buildings are made simply to offer a view. Long before airplanes, satellites and drones gave soldiers a modern eye in the sky, military watchtowers or observation posts were crucial for guarding against invading armies. Other towers were built specifically to watch for fires. Many Japanese cities built fire towers during the Edo period, between the 1600s and 1800s, and many geographically large countries like Canada, Russia and the United States built fire towers on top of hills and mountains to watch for forest fires. But in recent decades, more and more towers have been built as observatories so people can get up high and enjoy the view.

UNIVERSITY OF TOKYO ATACAMA OBSERVATORY

- *ALTITUDE: 18,503 feet (5,640 meters)*
- *HEIGHT: 605 feet (184 meters) • OPENED: 2009*
- *LOCATION: The summit of Cerro Chajnantor in Atacama Astronomical Park, Chile*

The highest astronomical observatory in the world is the University of Tokyo Atacama Observatory in Chile. It's located in a lava dome. It's one of the newest observatories in the world, but people have been gazing up at the stars for as long as humans have been alive. Ancient cultures built basic structures to track the movement of the sun and moon. The ancient Greeks built basic observatories, but Islamic scientists were the first to design anything resembling modern scientific observatories. Not long after Flemish instrument makers invented the optical telescope, the famous Italian Galileo Galilei (who was born in Pisa!) improved the design and pointed his own telescope up to the stars in 1609.

Seeing the Night Sky

Optical telescopes were very delicate, sensitive instruments, and protective dome-shaped observatories shielded them from the outside elements and a high vantage point. As scientists developed better telescopes to see stars and other planets, they realized they needed to build observatories at higher elevations, where they can gather better images because there is less light pollution and atmospheric interference. Today there are much larger, more scientifically advanced optical telescopes around the world, including the Atacama Observatory, a giant grouping atop Mauna Kea on the island of Hawaii and the colossal Gran Telescopio Canarias, a reflector telescope in the Canary Islands.

SPACE NEEDLE

- *HEIGHT: 605 feet (184 meters) to tip*
- *OBSERVATION DECK: 520 feet (158 meters)*
- *OPENED: 1962*
- *LOCATION: Seattle, Washington*

When Seattle was getting ready to host the 1962 world's fair, organizers knew they wanted to make an impression on visitors. Businessman Edward E. Carlson dreamed of a giant balloon floating over the fair, architect John Graham Jr. envisioned something that looked like a science-fiction drawing of a flying saucer, and fellow architect Victor Steinbrueck imagined a thin tower pinched in the middle like an hourglass. The Space Needle was the end result. When it was finished, it was the tallest American building west of the Mississippi River. The Space Needle was built out of steel and assembled in a tripod structure, with three long legs held together by 74,000 bolts. It took 400 days to build, and once complete, the tower was an instant blockbuster. More than 2.5 million people visited the Space Needle during the world's fair. Since then more than 60 million people have visited the iconic tower, which is now an official Seattle landmark.

Bird's-Eye View

The Space Needle took its cue from an observatory style that started in Germany in the 1950s. In Stuttgart, the Süddeutscher Rundfunk (South German Broadcasting Company) planned a 656-foot (200-meter)-tall iron-lattice transmission mast. But a famous structural engineer named Fritz Leonhardt convinced the company to build a new type of reinforced concrete tower instead, which could also hold an observation deck and restaurant. The company directors decided they could pay for the more expensive tower by charging admission, and they were right. The Fernsehturm Stuttgart reaches 712 feet (217 meters) above a wooded hill overlooking the city, and tourists flock there to take in the bird's-eye view.

Architects and other builders took notice of the Fernsehturm's successful ticket sales and design. Similar towers were built around the world in the decades that followed—in Canada, China, Iran, South Africa, New Zealand, the United States and elsewhere. Many offered views of big cities. Others presented natural wonders, like the Skylon Tower in Ontario, which gives tourists a stunning view of Niagara Falls.

The Space Needle offers 360-degree views of downtown Seattle from both indoor and outdoor viewing areas. It also features a revolving glass floor located 500 feet (152 meters) above ground.
JOE DANIEL PRICE/GETTY IMAGES

The Tokyo Skytree towers over its neighbors and many other tall buildings around the world. In fact, it's twice as high as the Eiffel Tower.
VLADIMIR ZAKHAROV/GETTY IMAGES

TOKYO SKYTREE

- **HEIGHT TO TIP: 2,080 feet (634 meters)**
- **TOP OF ROOF HEIGHT: 1,624 feet (495 meters)**
- **OPENED: 2012**
- **LOCATION: Tokyo, Japan**

Fifty years after the Space Needle was finished, a much taller tripod observation tower opened to the public on the other side of the Pacific Ocean. When it was finished, the Tokyo Skytree was the tallest tower in the world, and the second-tallest building. Like so many others, the Tokyo Skytree was built as both a communications tower and an observatory. In fact, the tower has two observatories. The lower one sits on top of the tripod structure at 1,148 feet (350 meters) and can hold up to 2,000 people. Above the lower observatory the tower changes shape and rises as a cylinder. At 1,480 feet (450 meters) above the ground it meets the upper observatory, which can accommodate 900 people.

When the weather is good, the observatory gives visitors a breathtaking view of Mount Fuji. It also offers a commanding perspective of the Tokyo skyline, both because of its height and because part of the floor is made of glass! The glass is incredibly thick and designed with safety in mind. The Tokyo Skytree is an engineering marvel, but it isn't the highest public observation deck in the world. That record belongs to the Shanghai Tower.

Seismic Safety

The Tokyo Skytree was designed with earthquakes in mind, as Japan is one of the most seismically active countries on Earth. Thanks to technologies like shock absorbers and vibration dampers, engineers say it will withstand a major quake.

SHANGHAI TOWER

When the Burj Khalifa opened, paying customers could ride the express elevators to the 148th floor and the top observation deck—more than 300 feet (91 meters) higher than the upper observation deck on the Skytree. But while the Burj Khalifa is the world's tallest building, it doesn't have the highest observatory. Visitors to the observation deck at the top of the Shanghai Tower peer down at the street 1,843 feet (562 meters) below them. They can see the flowing water of the Huangpu River, winding its way gracefully through one of the world's largest cities. And they can look down—yes, *down*—on the tops of some of the world's tallest buildings, including the Shanghai World Financial Center, the Oriental Pearl Tower and the Jin Mao Tower. Now that's a view to remember!

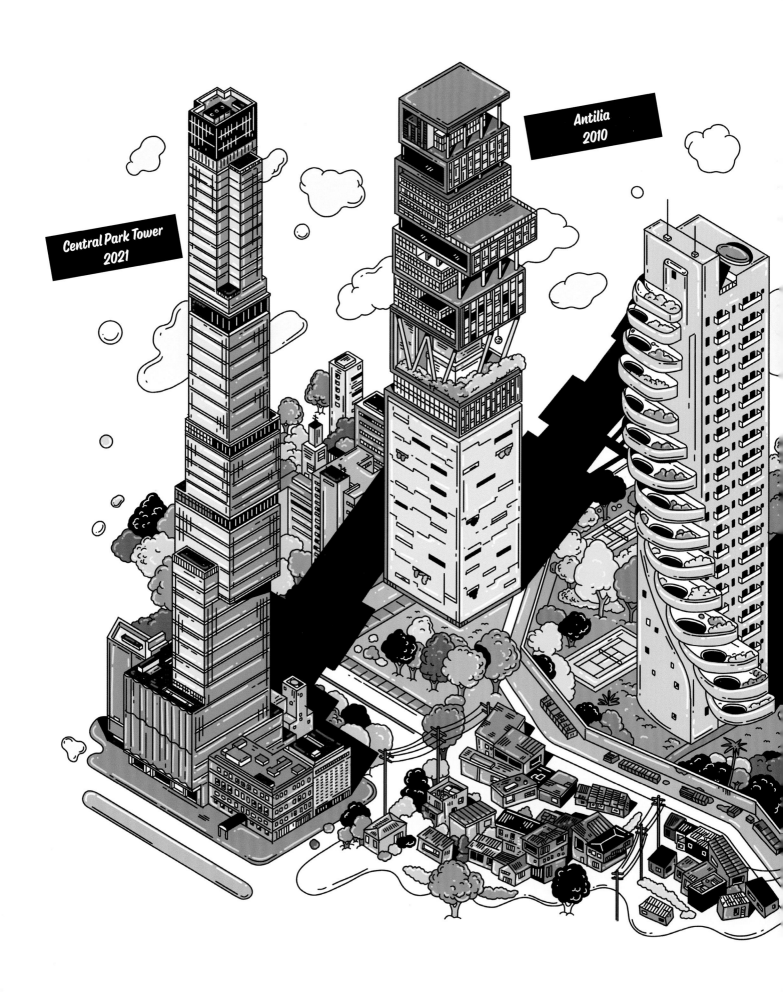

Central Park Tower
2021

Antilia
2010

Condomínio Penthouse
1974

Nine
LUXURY

CREATING EXTRAVAGANT HOMES HIGH IN THE SKY

If millions of average people will pay money to visit sky-high observatories, what will millionaires and billionaires pay to buy sky-high homes? The short answer is, a lot. And as more super-rich people decide they'd like to live high in the sky, more builders are giving them what they want. In many cases, people want a whole floor to themselves in order to enjoy views on all sides. Or maybe several whole floors. As a result, some of the newest residential towers are taller and skinnier than ever. Nowhere is this more apparent than in New York City, near Central Park. It's a part of Manhattan some locals now call Billionaires' Row.

CENTRAL PARK TOWER

- **HEIGHT:** 1,550 feet (472 meters) to top of building
- **YEAR FINISHED:** 2021
- **LOCATION:** New York City
- **FLOORS:** 98 habitable

By 2020, three of the five tallest buildings in New York stood on Billionaires' Row. Central Park Tower was the tallest when it was finished and cost an estimated $3 billion to build. Its apartments are large and luxurious, with leather walls, stone floors, bronze doorframes and many other fineries. But the views are what really sell these homes. And the heavenly combination of luxury and views doesn't come cheap—the buildings on Billionaires' Row are some of the most expensive residential properties in the world. In 2015 billionaire Michael Dell bought the top two stories of the One57 building for a little more than $100 million!

Super Thin Steinway Tower

Apart from being incredibly tall, these new ultra-luxury residential towers are incredibly thin. Steinway Tower— also known as 111 West 57th—is 1,425 feet (435 meters) tall but only 60 feet (18 meters) wide. That makes it the thinnest ultra-luxury supertall skyscraper—because it's nearly 24 times taller than its base! Structural engineers call this *slenderness*, and it refers to the ratio of the building's height to its footprint. If a building is more than 10 times as high as it is wide, it is considered a slender skyscraper. In contrast, the Empire State Building, is only about three times longer than the length of its base on the ground and is not considered slender.

Gigantic Pencils

These pencil-shaped towers have started rising as building developers buy something called air rights. Many years ago New York City established tower-height limits, but it also allowed owners of shorter buildings to sell the height they were not using to property owners who wanted to build higher than the limit. This enabled the builders of 111 West 57th Street to go higher, because they purchased the air rights of the historic Steinway Hall next door.

Steinway Hall

This iconic limestone building dates back to the 1920s. The famous Steinway pianos were sold here, and it also served as a concert venue. Steinway Hall is now a famous New York landmark—and it's only 10 stories tall. The builders of the new tower next door purchased the height Steinway Hall wasn't using, which meant Steinway Tower could be taller.

Towers can also go higher in some locations if they're skinnier because they stretch out the maximum amount of floor space that's allowed for the building over more floors. That means more sky-high views at sky-high prices.

BUILDING BLOCKS

THE SETBACK

A certain amount of open space is required around any building. But upper portions of tall buildings must be set back farther from the street than the base of the building to allow more light to reach the street and lower floors. Setback zoning laws have created a classic style of skyscraper that gets thinner as it gets higher.

ANTILIA

- *HEIGHT: 568 feet (173 meters) to top of building*
- *OPENED: 2010*
- *LOCATION: Mumbai*
- *FLOORS: 27*

While superrich buyers snap up homes in New York towers, billionaires in other cities are simply building their own towers. India's richest man, Mukesh Ambani, had a 27-story luxury tower built for himself, his family and a few hundred employees. Indian newspapers reported he paid $2 billion US for it. Antilia includes a grand ballroom, a theater, six floors of parking, floating gardens, three heliports and many more luxuries.

Antilia made headlines, but millions of Indians were not impressed. The idea of one family building such a large, luxurious residence for just themselves and a few employees offended a lot of people in a country where millions of people live in makeshift dwellings in slums, surviving on the equivalent of a few dollars a day. Even other billionaires were offended. Ratan Tata, whose family owns many businesses, told the *Times of London* that the building lacked empathy for the poor. "This country needs people to allocate some of their enormous wealth to finding ways of mitigating the hardship that people have," he said.

CONDOMÍNIO PENTHOUSE

- OPENED: 1974
- LOCATION: São Paulo, Brazil
- FLOORS: 16
- APARTMENTS PER FLOOR: 1
- SWIMMING POOLS PER APARTMENT: 1

Luxury in the Face of Poverty

The controversy over ultra-luxury towers isn't confined to India. In Brazil, people have complained about fancy new skyscrapers that seem too tall and ostentatious. In São Paulo, there are many favelas—poor, crowded neighborhoods where people live in basic shacks. The Paraisópolis favela sits right next to a wealthy area called Morumbi, where many luxurious towers are located. One building, the Condomínio Penthouse, even has individual swimming pools on each balcony, which overlook shacks in Paraisópolis.

The capital city of Angola, in southern Africa, also has several buildings casting shadows on poor low-rise neighborhoods. The 35-floor IMOB Business Tower was completed in 2018. It's one of a growing number of attractive skyscrapers rising near the water in this busy port city—signs of the recent growth in the African economy. But to many of the city's poor, these tall offices, hotels and residential buildings stand as reminders of the divide between rich and poor.

Height Doesn't Have to Be Luxurious

We've seen that building higher and higher can alienate some people and make them feel they are being denied the prosperity that others enjoy. But tall buildings can also do the opposite. They can provide housing for hundreds of families in a space that would otherwise fit only a few families. If they're well designed, high-rises can lift more people out of poverty and give them a place they can afford to call home.

BUILDING BLOCKS

AIR-CONDITIONING

For thousands of years, humans used snow and ice to stay cool. It wasn't until the 1800s that mechanical cooling was invented, by compressing and liquefying ammonia. The first electrical air conditioner was built in 1902. The first high-rise office building to include air-conditioning was the 21-story Milam Building, which opened in San Antonio, TX, in 1928. Other buildings with it soon followed. But air-conditioning comes with a cost—the chemicals it uses are harmful to the environment. One chemical, Freon, is responsible for a lot of the depletion of the ozone layer and has been banned by many countries. But hydrofluorocarbons, or HFCs, are also harmful and are still used in millions of air conditioners. Many countries have promised to stop using them in the next few years.

Seoul Apartments

Moscow State University

Hong Kong High-Rises

Ten
EFFICIENCY

USING LESS LAND BY BUILDING UP

Most cities have at least a few high-rises, but the world's largest cities look like they have nothing else! With the world's population growing, tall towers can be the most efficient way to provide space for people without cutting down more forests or building on farmland. As the chapter on luxury showed, not every tall building is more efficient than low-rise houses. After all, one family doesn't need 27 floors! But tall buildings can be much more efficient than the Antilia. And they can provide much more housing on a single piece of land than single-family homes can.

Hong Kong skyscrapers during the nightly A Symphony of Lights show, which is organized by the Hong Kong Tourism Board.
JINGMIN310/DREAMSTIME.COM

HONG KONG

- **POPULATION:** More than 7 million
- **DENSITY:** More than 17,000 people per square mile (nearly 7,000 people per square kilometer)
- **HIGH-RISES:** More than 8,300 taller than 114 feet (35 meters) or 12 stories
- **SKYSCRAPERS:** More than 1,900 taller than 328 feet (100 meters)

Hong Kong is one of the most densely populated cities on Earth, and most of those people live on less than one-quarter of Hong Kong's land because of laws that protect forests, beaches and mountains. With so many people squeezed into such a small space, it was only natural that Hong Kong would grow up rather than out.

Hong Kong wasn't the first city to soar into the sky. When the Empire State Building rose above New York, buildings in Hong Kong were still relatively low. The tallest building at the time was the 13-story HSBC Building. But refugees poured in from China after World War II and the Chinese Communist Revolution, when Hong Kong was still a British colony. Housing was in short supply, and the situation got worse in 1954 when a big fire raced through Hong Kong *shantytowns*, leaving more than 50,000 people homeless. The government responded by erecting large buildings, including the Choi Hung Estate in 1964—a cluster of buildings that could house 43,000 people. Private owners followed suit in the 1950s and '60s, knocking down much shorter tenement houses to put up apartment blocks of 20 stories or more.

City in the Sky

Hong Kong has been rising ever since, and today it's very much a vertical city. Many of the public places typically situated at ground level in other cities are commonly found much higher in Hong Kong, such as restaurants, shops and gardens. It isn't strange for Hong Kong residents to meet a friend for lunch in a restaurant on the 22nd floor. There is little doubt that Hong Kong has used its land efficiently to provide housing. And while many people love their homes, some are crammed into tiny spaces, and life is very difficult.

Tiny Homes

Many poor families live in one-room apartments with only enough space for a bed, sink and cupboards. Some apartments are as small as 128 square feet (about 12 square meters), which is roughly the size of a garden shed in North America. Some live on their own in even smaller **cubicle homes**—sometimes called coffin homes—that are barely bigger than a single bed. These cramped spaces have led some people to wonder if Hong Kong is too efficient. With the majority of its land protected and its population increasing, Hong Kong may have to keep rising. There are already plans for the government to build another 280,000 homes in the 2020s and for private builders to add 180,000 more. But some people predict Hong Kong will need even more.

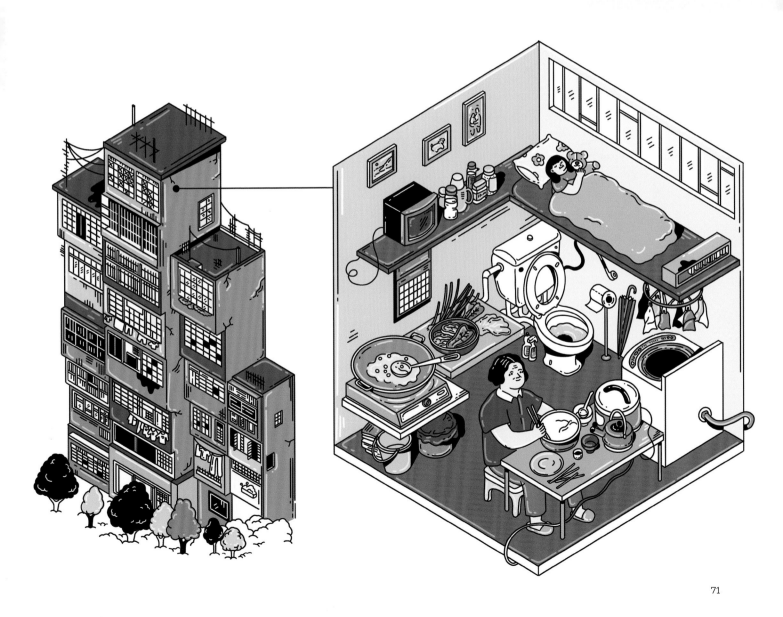

SEOUL

- *POPULATION: 10 million in city (21 million metro)*
- *DENSITY: 42,000 people per square mile (15,900 per square kilometer)*
- *HIGH-RISES: More than 18,000 · SKYSCRAPERS: 267 (in 2021)*

There is a similar city in the sky about 1,300 miles (2,000 kilometers) from Hong Kong. Seoul is the capital of South Korea and home to 10 million people. As in Hong Kong, most residents of Seoul live in apartment towers. Row after row of gray apartment buildings dominate the skyline. Some have compared Seoul to a giant game of dominoes, with long rows of tall, thin structures standing in uniform lines. They're not pleasing to everyone's eye, but they are an efficient use of space.

How High-Rises Lifted Korea Out of Poverty

At the end of the Korean War in the 1950s, only about 1 percent of Koreans lived in apartments. As South Korea started to rebuild, shantytowns were torn down to make way for new towers that could house more people. Some of the residents objected, and either didn't want to move into the new towers or couldn't afford to move into them. But many Koreans jumped at the chance to live in clean new apartments in the sky. Big public building projects started in the 1970s, and more than 60 percent of Koreans now live in apartment buildings.

Skyscrapers and high-rise apartment buildings overlook the Han River in the Yeongdeungpo-gu district of Seoul.
ALLAN BAXTER/GETTY IMAGES

MOSCOW

- *POPULATION: 12.5 million*
- *DENSITY: About 13,000 people per square mile (5,000 per square kilometer)*
- *HIGH-RISES: More than 12,000 · SKYSCRAPERS: 254 (in 2021)*

A similar transformation happened in Russia's largest city. Communist leaders started building towers in the 1920s as a response to a shortage of housing after the Russian Revolution. The Soviet government took possession of all land and built apartments where as many as seven families shared a kitchen. But Moscow really started to shoot up after World War II. The city had been heavily damaged, and more housing was needed desperately. Soviet dictator Joseph Stalin also decided Russia's capital city needed skyscrapers to impress foreign visitors, so he ordered the construction of a group of buildings called the Seven Sisters, a mix of Russian baroque and Gothic styles loosely based on New York's Municipal Building, as it was called then. The tallest is the 36-floor Moscow State University, which remained the tallest building in Europe for more than 30 years. Some of the other towers are used for housing, like the 32-story Kotelnicheskaya Embankment Building.

From Eye-Catching to Efficient

In the years that followed, however, the Soviet Union took a more practical approach to building homes for millions of people. Many houses were built with *prefabricated* walls so they could go up quickly and in great numbers. Thousands of these buildings have been torn down since the collapse of the Soviet Union, because they were not built to last long and many were seen as brutal, ugly structures. But these massive buildings made efficient use of space and time to provide tens of millions of Russians with much-needed housing.

Bahrain World Trade Center
2008

Brock Commons Tallwood House
2017

Manitoba Hydro Place
2009

Eastgate Centre
1996

Eleven
SUSTAINABILITY

CAN TALL BUILDINGS HELP US SAVE THE PLANET?

The world's population reached two billion people in the 1920s, when the Eiffel Tower was still the world's tallest structure. It had soared to seven billion by 2011, just after the completion of the Burj Khalifa. As we speed toward eight billion, our growing population places immense pressure on the planet. And as cities grow, there is increasing pressure to expand outward into surrounding wild spaces—the forests and farmlands needed for food, wildlife habitat and climate control. Tall buildings can help ease that pressure by allowing cities to grow up, not out.

The Bahrain World Trade Center towers are 50 stories tall. They are shaped like sails and can be seen from a great distance by boats on the Arabian Sea. But it was the building's environmentally friendly technologies that really caught the world's attention.

BUENA VISTA IMAGES/GETTY IMAGES

The 7,000 photovoltaic panels on the CIS Solar Tower in Manchester generate enough electricity to power 55 houses for a year, or make nine million cups of tea!

CHRISTOPHER FURLONG/GETTY IMAGES

BAHRAIN WORLD TRADE CENTER

- **HEIGHT:** *787 feet (240 meters)*
- **OPENED:** *2008*
- **LOCATION:** *Manama, Bahrain*
- **GREEN TECHNOLOGIES:** *Wind turbines, seawater cooling, shading measures, deep gravel roofs for insulation*

Some new buildings are shrinking their environmental footprint by using *renewable energy* like wind and solar power. Wind turbines are attached to both the Bahrain World Trade Center and the Shanghai Tower to take advantage of the strong winds near the top of the buildings. The turbines on the Shanghai Tower provide the electricity for the 22,000 LED lights on the outside of the building. The Shanghai Tower also has a transparent second skin that provides insulation between the air outside and the air inside the building, reducing the need for both heating and cooling. Around the world, some new towers will also have *solar panels* on their roofs and walls.

Sun Power

When the 25-story CIS Tower in Manchester, England, needed a face-lift, its service tower was covered in blue photovoltaic (solar) panels. Manchester has a lot of rainy days, but the panels still generate about 180,000 kilowatt-hours of electricity a year. The building is now known to many in Manchester as simply the Solar Tower. In the future, some towers might be completely covered in see-through solar-panel windows. As the technology improves, buildings will generate more of their own power, maybe even all of it.

MANITOBA HYDRO PLACE

- **HEIGHT:** 377 feet (115 meters)
- **OPENED:** 2009
- **LOCATION:** Winnipeg, Manitoba
- **GREEN TECHNOLOGIES:** Solar chimney, passive design, geothermal heating

The power of the sun can also be captured by a **solar chimney**. A Winnipeg office building called Manitoba Hydro Place uses a solar chimney that draws heat exhaust from upper floors in the winter and recirculates it to the underground parkade. It also uses it to preheat incoming air from outside. Architect Bruce Kuwabara calls that "the free heating of solar energy." In the summer, the solar chimney draws hot air to the top and out of the building.

Manitoba Hydro Place makes use of several green technologies, consuming 70 percent less energy than similar-sized buildings. The tower was built with a **geothermal heating** system that's connected to 280 thin holes (called boreholes) that reach 410 feet (125 meters) underground to bring the natural heat that's found in the earth up into the building.

It also was built using something called **passive design**, which makes sure the building faces the right direction to capture lots of sunlight in the cold winter months. Kuwabara calls Manitoba Hydro Place the most important building he and his team have ever designed. "It's not the height," he said. "It's the response to the environment."

The 23-story office building uses double glass walls for insulation and a design that takes full advantage of its surroundings to provide natural heat and light. It uses a lot less power than most buildings of a similar size.
MATT CORKUM / 500PX/GETTY IMAGES

HIGHLIGHTS

MATERIALS MATTER
The materials used to build a tower also affect its environmental footprint. Steel and concrete are incredibly strong, and they enabled the building of skyscrapers, but producing these materials creates nearly 10 percent of the world's fossil fuel emissions, according to some estimates. On top of that, many skyscrapers need a lot more energy to heat or cool their interiors than smaller buildings do. But builders, architects and engineers are developing new ways to shrink the environmental footprint of a building. Renewable materials like wood can be a better environmental choice if they are harvested responsibly—that means cutting some, but not all, trees in a *sustainably managed forest* to make beams. The wood in those beams also stores all the carbon that was sucked out of the atmosphere during the tree's lifetime. These improvements, combined with the fact that towers can house many more people than single-family homes, mean tall buildings can be good for the planet.

BROCK COMMONS TALLWOOD HOUSE
• *HEIGHT: 174 feet (53 meters) to top of building* • *OPENED: 2017*
• *LOCATION: Vancouver, British Columbia* • *GREEN TECHNOLOGY: Laminated wood*

At the University of British Columbia in Vancouver is an 18-floor student residence called Brock Commons Tallwood House that was built out of wood. Tallwood House includes **laminated wood** floors that are connected with steel brackets to laminated wood columns. One of the reasons wood wasn't allowed for tall buildings in the past was the worry about fire. It's true that wood can burn faster than other materials. But scientists, firefighters and safety experts tested the heavy laminated timbers and concluded the outside of the timbers would get charred by flames but would not burn easily because they are so thick. The wooden walls are also covered by three or four layers of fire-resistant gypsum wallboard, and the building contains a backup water supply in case the power goes out.

Going Green
Architects from Tokyo to Toronto are now planning high-rises made with laminated timber. In Sweden, Anders Berensson Architects has designed a housing development in Stockholm that will include 5,000 homes in 31 engineered-wood towers. "Wood is the building material that releases the least carbon dioxide in today's construction industry," the architects concluded, "and is therefore the obvious choice."

There are more things that can make tall buildings sustainable, and many are relatively simple. Using local materials instead of shipping them around the world can reduce the carbon footprint in construction. Once a tower is built, adding vegetation can also help. The One Central Park building in Sydney and the Oasia Hotel in Singapore both have outdoor plants that provide shade for the building, which helps reduce its energy use and keep it cool. Some buildings collect rainwater from the roof. Others have floor-to-ceiling window glazing that keeps more heat inside in the winter, reducing the energy needed to keep offices warm. And some use natural cooling systems.

When Tallwood House opened, it was the tallest mass timber structure in the world. It now provides housing for more than 400 university students.
BRUDDER PRODUCTIONS, COURTESY NATURALLYWOOD.COM

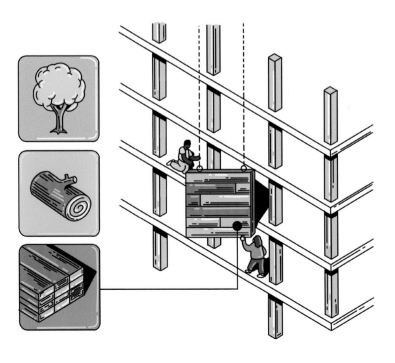

EASTGATE CENTRE
· FLOORS: 9 · OPENED: 1996 · LOCATION: Harare, Zimbabwe
· GREEN TECHNOLOGY: Biomimicry

In Harare, the capital city of Zimbabwe, the Eastgate Centre building features an ingenious design based on nature to heat and cool the building. This amazing building isn't the world's tallest, but it reached new heights of sustainable design. It has no traditional heating or cooling systems but stays cool year-round by using traditional Zimbabwean methods of masonry and by copying the design of African termite mounds. Yes, termite mounds! This green technology is called *biomimicry*.

The insects build giant mud piles for themselves (like termite skyscrapers), with tunnels on the inside and air vents outside. By opening and closing the vents, the termites allow cold air in from below when the temperature is cooler and allow the hot air to be drawn out the top. That helps maintain a steady temperature inside the mound. Architect Mick Pearce worked with engineers to copy this natural phenomenon and used adjustable window blinds and extra walls to provide shade. As a result the building uses only 10 percent of the electricity of a similar building with air-conditioning.

A Fungal Future?

Some architects and engineers are working on even more sustainable ways to build. Phil Ayres, an architect in Denmark, thinks mushrooms might help. Yes, mushrooms! Ayres and a team of researchers are looking at mycelium, the thin fibers that look like spiderwebs under a fungus. Mycelium grows quickly and can be shaped as it grows, like wet concrete. This research may find that fungus is a good building material—one that's much gentler on the planet.

So maybe in the future, tall buildings will be able to generate all their power from the sun and wind. Maybe they'll even be able to make more than they need and share it with others! We aren't there yet, but as the history of skyscrapers shows, architects and engineers have innovated and designed their way to new heights time and time again. Perhaps they can be part of finding the world's fix for climate change.

BIGGER AND BIGGER ENVIRONMENTAL FOOTPRINTS

A 2019 study by BC Hydro found that new buildings in Vancouver and Victoria use about twice as much power as similar high-rises built in the 1980s, and almost four times more than low-rises built at the same time. One of the reasons is that shared luxuries in the newer buildings, like hot tubs, pools and party rooms, consume a lot of power. Another reason is that lighting, heating and cooling in many parts of high-rises remain on around the clock, while people who live in smaller homes turn them off to save power and money. Residents and managers of new high-rises can help reduce energy consumption by shading windows, using fans and installing automatic sensors to turn off lights and heating when parts of the building are empty.

Glossary

arched—formed in an arch, which is a curved structure that spans an opening and supports the weight of a roof, wall or bridge above it. Brick arches were built as early as 2000 BCE in Mesopotamia. Leonardo da Vinci famously said, "An arch consists of two weaknesses which, leaning one against the other, make a strength."

architect—a professional who designs and draws up plans for a building and decides what it will look like

art deco—a decorative style of art and architecture that was popular in the 1920s and '30s, featuring bold shapes and colors on modern materials like steel and plastic

beam—a long piece of wood, iron or steel that lies horizontally across a building to support the floor above or the roof. Steel beams are often called *girders*.

Buddhists—followers of Buddhism, a religion that was started in India by the Buddha, also known as Siddhārtha Gautama, and later spread around the world

column—an upright pillar or post made of stone, concrete, wood or steel that serves as a support. Like the legs of a table, which transfer the weight of the tabletop and everything on it to the floor, columns transfer the upper weight of a building down to the ground.

concrete—a building material composed of sand, gravel, cement and water, which can be poured wet and solidifies to become as hard as stone

cubicle homes—tiny homes in which the bed, toilet and kitchen are in one tiny space that is almost not big enough for a person to stretch out their legs. Also called *coffin homes*

engineer—an expert in the technical and structural elements of building, whose work includes calculating how strong walls need to be and what types of materials to use

environmental footprint—the effect that a building, person, company or activity has on the planet and its natural resources

geothermal heating—the hot water and steam stored underground, beneath the earth's surface, which can be turned into electricity. Geothermal power stations can be placed inside buildings to provide electricity for the building itself.

Gothic—an architectural style that was popular in Europe in the Middle Ages. It featured large, cavernous stone spaces with pointed arches and stained glass.

Great Depression—a severe economic downturn in the 1930s that started in the United States and spread around the world, causing millions of people to lose money, jobs and their homes

Kufic—an early form of Arabic writing, famous for its angular style. Architecturally, it was used for decorative inscriptions on walls.

laminated wood—layers of wood that are glued together to form thicker, stronger beams and boards. Also known as *engineered wood*, or *mass timber*

masonry—a way of building walls and other structures by laying bricks or other building blocks and binding them together with mortar

passive design—a method of design in which a building is laid out so that the windows, walls and floors circulate, collect, reflect and store solar heat in the winter and reject that heat in the summer

prefabricated—describes parts of a building that are made at a factory or other location and then moved and installed quickly at the building site

reefs—underwater ridges of jagged rock or coral just under the surface of the water

renewable energy—natural sources of electricity that come from nature and can be replenished again and again, like wind and solar power

Seven Wonders of the Ancient World—the most remarkable structures of the ancient world, as compiled and recorded by ancient Greek authors more than 2,000 years ago

shantytowns—improvised settlements of basic shacks, often made by people with nowhere else to go, and usually lacking safe sanitation, water and electricity

skyscraper—a building with continuously habitable space for more than 40 floors that is also taller than 492 feet (150 meters). The term dates back to the 1880s, when it referred to buildings of 10 to 20 floors.

solar chimney—a vertical airway on the side of a building that allows buildings to stay cool or warm by using the natural tendency of hot air to rise and cold air to sink. Also known as a *thermal chimney*

solar panels—flat panels of photovoltaic cells that absorb sunlight and convert it into electricity for lighting, heating and cooling systems, and other things that require power

spire—a cone or pyramid that sits on top of a building, like a hat on a person's head. Spires are found on many churches and some skyscrapers as well.

sustainably managed forest—a forest that is managed in a way that balances human needs with the health of the forest habitat. Some trees are allowed to be cut for construction and economic benefit, but others are preserved to maintain the forest's biodiversity.

temperature inversion—a weather phenomenon in which cold air is trapped beneath a layer of warmer air, making the air up high warmer than the air on the ground. This is the opposite of normal conditions, where air temperature goes down as altitude increases.

World War I—a global war that started in Europe in 1914 and continued until 1918. Also known as the First World War and the Great War

World War II—a global war that took place between 1939 and 1945. It was the most damaging war in history and resulted in the deaths of tens of millions of people.

Resources

PRINT

Dillon, Patrick. *The Story of Buildings: From the Pyramids to the Sydney Opera House and Beyond.* Illus. Stephen Biesty. Candlewick, 2014.

Macaulay, David. *Building Big.* HMH Books for Young Readers, 2004.

Paxmann, Christine. *From Mud Huts to Skyscrapers: Architecture for Children.* Illus. Anne Ibelings. Prestel Junior, 2012.

Wilkinson, Philip. *Amazing Buildings.* Illus. Paolo Donati. DK Limited, 1993.

ONLINE

Big Ben: parliament.uk/bigben

Burj Khalifa: burjkhalifa.ae/en/the-tower/facts-figures

CN Tower: cntower.ca/history-and-science/design-science-and-innovation

Eiffel Tower: toureiffel.paris/en

Empire State Building: esbnyc.com

Fernsehturm Stuttgart: fernsehturm-stuttgart.de/en/der-turm

Great Pyramid of Giza: worldhistory.org/Great_Pyramid_of_Giza

High-rise buildings: emporis.com

Leaning Tower of Pisa: towerofpisa.org

Lighthouse of Alexandria: ancient.eu/Lighthouse_of_Alexandria

Manitoba Hydro Place:
   hydro.mb.ca/corporate/history/mh_place_design_and_construction

NASA Vehicle Assembly Building: nasa.gov/content/vehicle-assembly-building

Skyscrapers around the world: skyscrapercenter.com

Slender skyscrapers: old.skyscraper.org

Space Needle: spaceneedle.com

Tokyo Skytree: tokyo-skytree.jp/en

UNESCO World Heritage in Danger: whc.unesco.org/en/danger

Acknowledgments

I've been fortunate to have so many books, articles and websites at my disposal to research the facts, figures and stories behind some of the world's tallest buildings. But sometimes you need to talk to real people, especially people who are experts in their fields. I'm particularly grateful to architect Bruce Kuwabara, who is a founding partner of the architectural firm KPMB and who took the time to talk to me about Manitoba Hydro Place and other aspects of sustainable building design. I'm also grateful to structural engineer Ronald Hamburger, who is a past president of the National Council of Structural Engineers Associations and a senior principal at Simpson Gumpertz & Heger (SGH). I also benefited greatly from visiting the Skyscraper Museum in New York—I found the staff there very helpful and informative.

I'm also thankful to everyone at Orca Book Publishers who made this book possible, especially Kirstie Hudson for editing the book and encouraging me to write in the first place, and both Andrew Wooldridge and Ruth Linka for choosing to publish the book!

Index   *Page numbers in **bold** indicate an image caption.*

Gregor Craigie is a writer and journalist. He wakes up at 3:45 every weekday morning to talk on CBC Radio in Victoria, British Columbia. Despite the early hours, Gregor loves his job because he gets to ask questions and write for a living. Before his current job at the Canadian Broadcasting Corporation, he worked for the BBC World Service in London and traveled to several different countries, telling stories for radio listeners. *Why Humans Build Up* is his first book for kids.

Kathleen Fu is a Canadian illustrator based in Toronto with a background in fine art, architecture and urban design. She is a graduate of the University of Waterloo School of Architecture and her current work is heavily inspired by her time studying architecture, city life and storytelling. She enjoys creating intricate illustrations with a Where's Waldo-esque style, injecting each piece with as many unique characters and different shapes as possible. Her work has been published in the *New York Times*, *Reader's Digest*, the *Globe and Mail*, *The Walrus* and many other publications.

THE MORE YOU KNOW
THE MORE YOU GROW

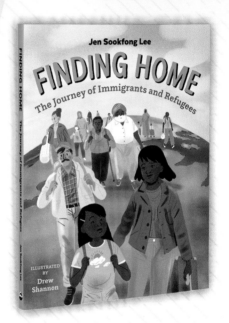

Jen Sookfong Lee

FINDING HOME
The Journey of Immigrants and Refugees

ILLUSTRATED BY
Drew Shannon

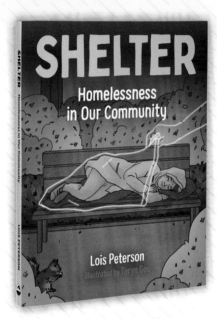

SHELTER
Homelessness in Our Community

Lois Peterson

Illustrated by Taryn Gee

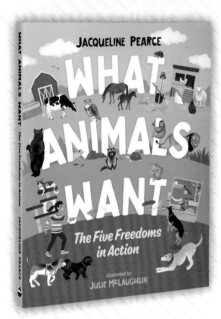

JACQUELINE PEARCE

WHAT ANIMALS WANT
The Five Freedoms in Action

illustrated by
JULIE McLAUGHLIN

Megan Clendenan
illustrated by Julie McLaughlin

Fresh Air, Clean Water
Our Right to a Healthy Environment

SOLUTIONS not POLLUTION!

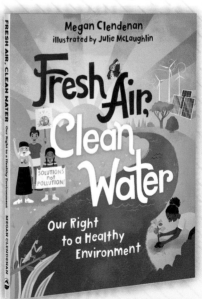

WHY HUMANS WORK
How Jobs Shape Our Lives and Our World

Monique Polak
illustrated by Suharu Ogawa

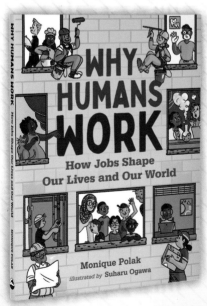

Tanya Lloyd Kyi

BETTER CONNECTED

Julia Kyi

illustrated by Vivian Rosas

How Girls Are Using Social Media for Good

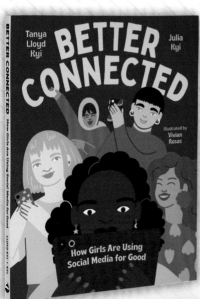

SAVE NATURAL HABITATS!!

WHAT'S THE BIG IDEA?

The **Orca Think** series introduces us to the issues making headlines in the world today. It encourages us to question, connect and take action for a better future. With those tools we can all become better citizens. Now that's smart thinking!

PETITION